I0500582

U.S. Fish & Wildlife Service

Comprehensive Conservation Plan

John H. Chafee National Wildlife Refuge

Prepared by:

Nancy McGarigal, Refuge Planner
Northeast Regional Office, Division of Planning
300 Westgate Center Drive
Hadley, MA 01035
(413) 253-8562

Local contact:

Charlie Vandemoer, Refuge Manager
3769 D Old Post Road
Charlestown, RI 02813
(401) 364-9124

Cover photo: Black duck, USFWS photo

May 2002

This goose, designed by J.N. "Ding" Darling, has become a symbol of the National Wildlife Refuge System.

The *U.S. Fish & Wildlife Service* is the principal federal agency responsible for conserving, protecting, and enhancing fish and wildlife and their habitats for the continuing benefit of the American people. The Service manages the 93-million acre National Wildlife Refuge System comprised of more than 500 national wildlife refuges and thousands of waterfowl production areas. It also operates 65 national fish hatcheries and 78 ecological services field stations. The agency enforces federal wildlife laws, manages migratory bird populations, restores nationally significant fisheries, conserves and restores wildlife habitat such as wetlands, administers the Endangered Species Act, and helps foreign governments with their conservation efforts. It also oversees the Federal Aid program which distributes hundreds of millions of dollars in excise taxes on fishing and hunting equipment to state wildlife agencies.

Comprehensive Conservation Plans provide long term guidance for management decisions; set forth goals, objectives, and strategies needed to accomplish refuge purposes; and, identify the Service's best estimate of future needs. These plans detail program planning levels that are sometimes substantially above current budget allocations and, as such, are primarily for Service strategic planning and program prioritization purposes. The plans do not constitute a commitment for staffing increases, operational and maintenance increases, or funding for future land acquisition.

Comprehensive Conservation Plan Approval
for John H. Chafee National Wildlife Refuge at Pettaquamscutt Cove

Submitted by:

(signature)   6/21/02

Charles E. Vandemoer,   Date
Refuge Manager,
Rhode Island NWR Complex

Approved by:

(signature)   7/15/02

Richard W. Dyer,   Date
Refuge Supervisor, North
National Wildlife Refuge System

Approved by:

(signature)   8/9/02

Anthony D. Léger,   Date
Northeast Regional Chief,
National Wildlife Refuge System

Final approval:

(signature)   8/13/02

Dr. Mamie A. Parker,   Date
Regional Director, Region 5
U.S. Fish and Wildlife Service

Table of Contents

John H. Chafee National Wildlife Refuge CCP

Chapter 1

Wood ducks
USFWS photo

Introduction and Background

- Refuge Overview
- Purpose of and Need for a CCP
- Mission
- Refuge Purpose
- National and Regional Mandates Guiding this CCP
- Existing Partnerships

Introduction

This Comprehensive Conservation Plan (CCP) is the culmination of a planning process that began in February 1998. Numerous meetings with the public, the state, and conservation partners were held to identify and evaluate management alternatives. A draft Comprehensive Conservation Plan and Environmental Assessment (CCP/EA) was distributed in December 2000. This CCP presents the management goals, objectives, and strategies that we believe will best achieve our vision for the refuge, contribute to the National Wildlife Refuge System Mission, achieve refuge purposes and legal mandates, and serve the American public.

Refuge Overview

Originally established as Pettaquamscutt Cove National Wildlife Refuge, John H. Chafee National Wildlife Refuge (Chafee Refuge) is the newest addition to the Refuge Complex. The refuge is located in the Towns of South Kingstown and Narragansett, Washington County, RI, and centered in the community of Middlebridge (see maps 1-1 and 1-2). The refuge is mainly surrounded by private land. Most of its parcels border the Narrow River, a navigable public waterway.

In 1988, Senator John H. Chafee proposed legislation designating 600 acres of Pettaquamscutt Cove and its associated uplands for the protection of black ducks, shorebirds, and other waterfowl. In 1996, another bill revised the refuge acquisition boundary to include the 128-acre "Foddering Farm Acres," purchased in 1997. In 1999, Congress recognized Senator John H. Chafee's significant contributions to natural resource protection by renaming Pettaquamscutt Cove Refuge the "John H. Chafee at Pettaquamscutt Cove National Wildlfie Refuge". The 2002 Land Protection Plan (Appendix E) expanded the acquisition boundary by 878 acres. The refuge currently owns 329 acres within a 1,342-acre refuge acquisition boundary.

The Purpose of and Need for a CCP

Developing a CCP is vital to refuge management. The purpose of the CCP is to provide strategic management direction over the next 15 years, by…

- Providing a clear statement of desired future conditions for habitat, wildlife, visitor services, and facilities;

- Providing refuge neighbors, visitors, and partners with a clear understanding of the reasons for management actions;

- Ensuring refuge management reflects the policies and goals of the Refuge System and legal mandates;

- Ensuring the compatibility of current and future public use;

- Providing long-term continuity and direction for refuge management; and

- Providing direction for staffing, operations, maintenance, and developing budget requests.

Map 1-1

Rhode Island National Wildlife Refuge Complex
U.S. Fish & Wildlife Service Current Ownership

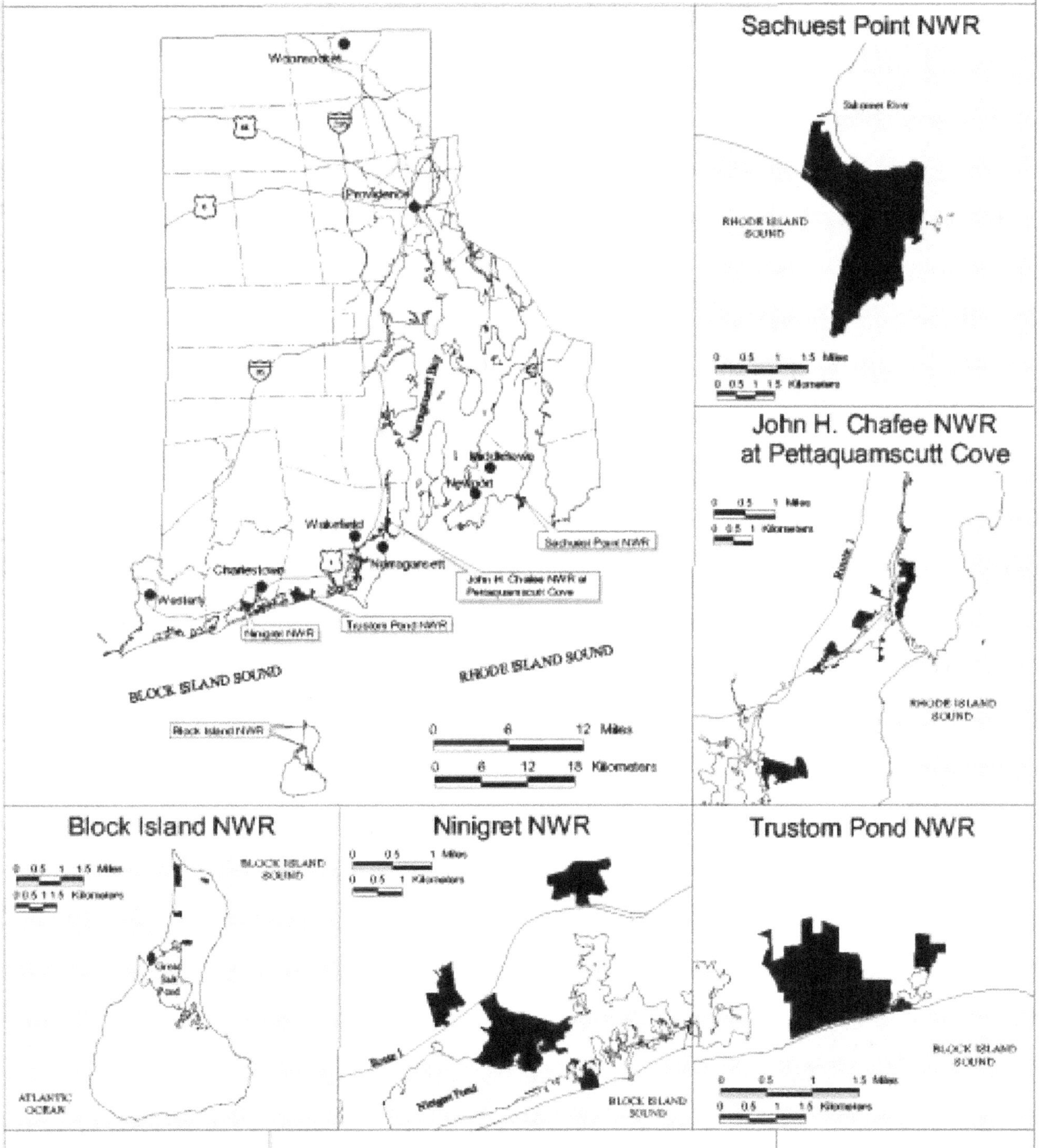

Sachuest Point NWR

John H. Chafee NWR
at Pettaquamscutt Cove

Block Island NWR

Ninigret NWR

Trustom Pond NWR

Data Sources:

Rhode Island State and Town
Boundaries from MassGIS
USFWS Refuge Boundaries
USGS 1:100,000 Roads

Map prepared for RI Complex Comprehensive
Conservation Plan, March 2002.

Block Island: Established in 1973; currently 102 acres
John H. Chafee: Established in 1988; currently 322 acres
Ninigret: Established in 1970; currently 713 acres
Sachuest Point: Established in 1973; currently 242 acres
Trustom Pond: Established in 1973; currently 659 acres

*Acreage figures are approximate.

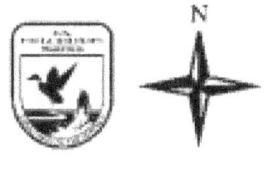

Block Island National Wildlife Refuge
Current Ownership and Approved Acquisition Boundary
Rhode Island NWR Complex Comprehensive Conservation Plan

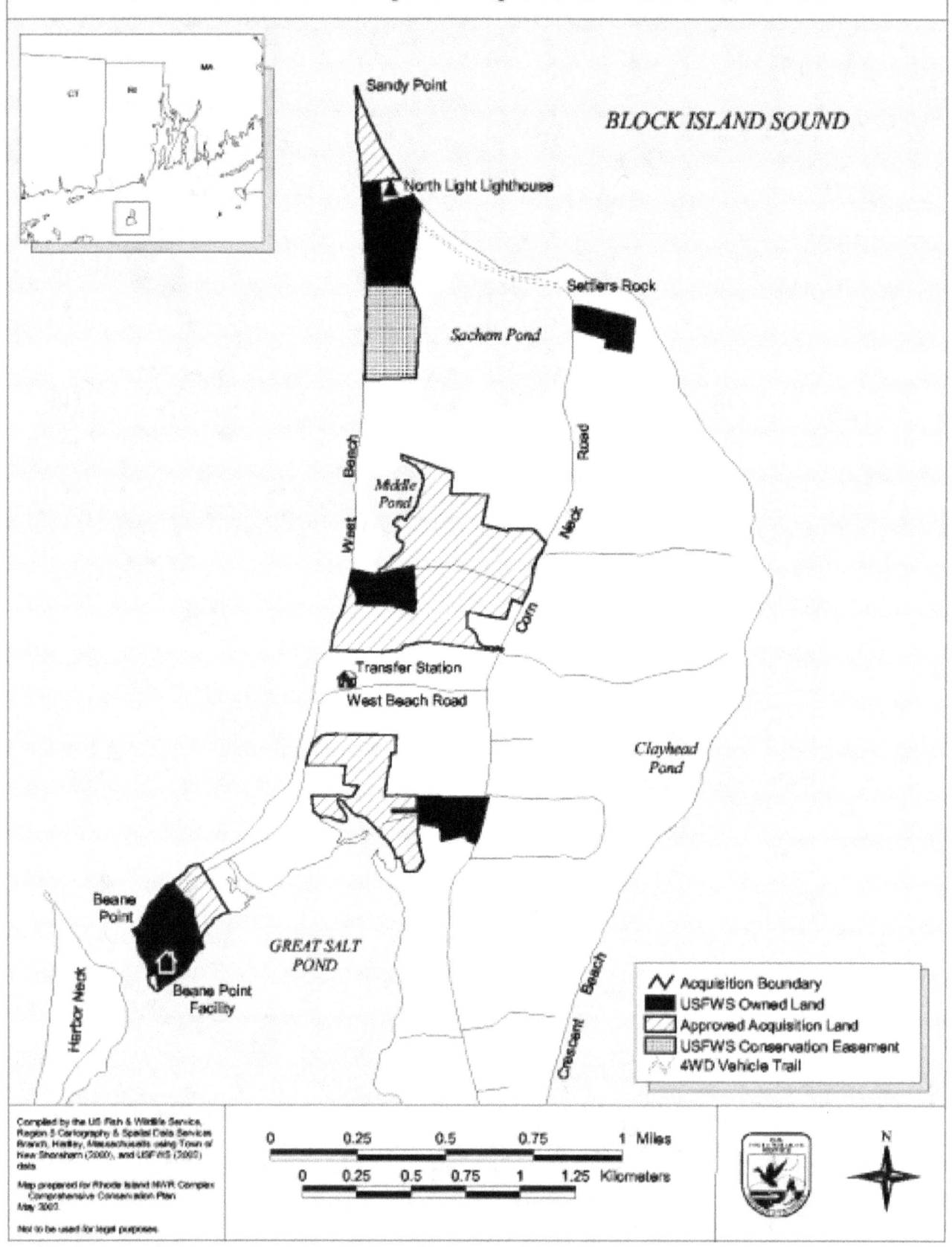

BLOCK ISLAND SOUND

Sandy Point

North Light Lighthouse

Settlers Rock

Sachem Pond

West Beach

Neck Road

Middle Pond

Corn Neck Road

Transfer Station

West Beach Road

Clayhead Pond

Beane Point

GREAT SALT POND

Beane Point Facility

Harbor Neck

Crescent Beach

Legend
- /\/ Acquisition Boundary
- ■ USFWS Owned Land
- ▨ Approved Acquisition Land
- ▦ USFWS Conservation Easement
- /\ 4WD Vehicle Trail

0   0.25   0.5   0.75   1 Miles

0   0.25   0.5   0.75   1   1.25 Kilometers

N

Compiled by the US Fish & Wildlife Service,
Region 5 Cartography & Spatial Data Services
Branch, Hadley, Massachusetts using Town of
New Shoreham (2000), and USFWS (2000)
data.

Map prepared for Rhode Island NWR Complex
Comprehensive Conservation Plan.
May 2002.

Not to be used for legal purposes.

The need to develop a CCP for Chafee Refuge is two-fold. First, the 1997 National Wildlife Refuge System Improvement Act (Refuge Improvement Act) requires that all national wildlife refuges have a CCP in place by 2012 to help fulfill the mission of the Refuge System. Second, the refuge lacks a master plan that establishes priorities and ensures consistent, integrated management among the five refuges in the Rhode Island Refuge Complex.

The U.S. Fish and Wildlife Service and its Mission

"...working with others, to conserve, protect and enhance fish wildlife, and plants and their habitats for the continuing benefit of the American people."

– Mission, U.S. Fish & Wildlife Service

The Service, part of the Department of the Interior, manages national wildlife refuges and national fish hatcheries. By law, Congress entrusts the following federal trust resources to the Service for conservation and protection: migratory birds and fish, endangered species, inter-jurisdictional fish, wetlands, and certain marine mammals. The Service also enforces federal wildlife laws and international treaties on importing and exporting wildlife, assists with state fish and wildlife programs, and helps other countries develop wildlife conservation programs.

The National Wildlife Refuge System and its Mission

"...to administer a national network of lands and waters for the conservation, management, and where appropriate, restoration of the fish, wildlife, and plant resources and their habitats within the United States for the benefit of present and future generations of Americans."

– Refuge System Mission, Refuge Improvement Act; Public Law 105-57

The Refuge System is the world's largest collection of lands and waters set aside specifically for conserving wildlife and protecting ecosystems. More than 525 national wildlife refuges, in every state and a number of U.S. Territories, protect more than 93 million acres. More than 34 million visitors annually hunt, fish, observe and photograph wildlife, or participate in environmental education and interpretive activities on refuges.

In 1997, Congress passed the National Wildlife Refuge System Improvement Act, establishing a unifying mission for the Refuge System, and a new process for determining compatible public use activities on refuges. It also requires that we prepare a CCP for each refuge. The act states that, first and foremost, the Refuge System must focus on wildlife conservation. It further states that the mission of the Refuge System, coupled with the purpose(s) for which each refuge was established, will provide the foundation for management direction for each refuge.

On public use, the act declares that all existing or proposed public uses must be compatible with each refuge's purpose. It highlights six wildlife-dependent public uses as priorities that all CCPs must evaluate: environmental education and interpretation, fishing, hunting, and wildlife observation and photography. Each refuge manager determines the compatibility of an activity by evaluating its potential impact on refuge resources, insuring that the activity supports the Refuge System mission, and ensuring that the activity does not materially detract from or interfere with the refuge purpose.

Refuge Purpose

The establishment purposes for Chafee Refuge are:

(1) To protect and enhance the populations of black duck and other waterfowl, geese, shorebirds, terns, wading birds, and other wildlife using the refuge;

(2) To provide for the conservation and management of fish and wildlife within the refuge;

(3) To fulfill international treaty obligations of the U.S. respecting fish and wildlife;

(4) To provide opportunities for scientific research, environmental education, and wildlife-oriented recreation.

– 102 Stat. 3177, Nov. 5, 1988 (Public Law 100-610)

National and Regional Mandates Guiding this CCP

This section highlights Service policy, legal mandates, and existing resource plans, arranged from the national to the local level, that directly influenced development of this CCP.

The *Digest of Federal Resource Laws of Interest to the USFWS* lists the various federal laws, Executive Orders, treaties, interstate compacts, and regulations on conserving and protecting natural and cultural resources (online at http://laws.fws.gov/lawsdigest/indx.html). The Service Manual and Refuge Manual contain Service policies and guidance on planning and day-to-day refuge management. The draft CCP/EA was written to fulfill compliance with National Environmental Policy Act of 1969 (NEPA)

North American Waterfowl Management Plan (May 14, 1986)

Black duck. *USFWS photo.*

This plan outlines the strategy among the United States, Canada, and Mexico to restore waterfowl populations by protecting, restoring, and enhancing habitat within 11 U.S. Joint Venture Regional Areas and three species Joint Ventures: Arctic Goose, Black Duck, and Sea Duck. Partnerships among federal, state and provincial governments, tribal nations, local businesses, conservation organizations, and individual citizens protect that habitat. The Refuge Complex lies within the Atlantic Coast Joint Venture, which has identified 13 priority focus areas totaling 3,226 acres of both wetlands and adjacent uplands for protection in Rhode Island (Atlantic Coast Joint Venture 1988). Three priority focus areas in the Refuge Complex are Trustom Pond, Ninigret Pond, and the Pettaquamscutt (Narrow) River.

Since black ducks winter in Rhode Island, the goals and objectives of the Black Duck Joint Venture apply to managing the Refuge Complex. The Black Duck Joint Venture has identified the coastal salt marsh habitats along the mid-upper Atlantic coast as very important wintering habitat.

Partners In Flight Landbird Conservation Plan: Physiographic Area 9, Southern New England (draft, October 2000)

In 1990, Partners in Flight (PIF) was conceived as a voluntary, international coalition of government agencies, conservation organizations, academic institutions, private industry, and other citizens dedicated to reversing the downward trends of declining species and "keeping common birds common." The foundation of PIF's long-term strategy for bird conservation is a series of scientifically based Landbird Conservation Plans. The goal of each PIF Landbird Conservation Plan is to ensure long term maintenance of healthy populations of native landbirds.

The Partners in Flight Program is developing a plan for the Southern New England Physiographic Area, using existing data on habitat loss, landbird population trends, and the vulnerability of species and habitats to threats, to rank the conservation priority of landbird species. The plan will identify focal species for each habitat type from which population and habitat objectives and conservation actions will be determined. We utilized this draft document for the list of priority species to consider in management. A revised draft of the plan was released in October 2000, and we will use the final plan, when finished, to further guide management.

Connecticut River/Long Island Sound Ecosystem Priorities, 1997

During the last decade, we have emphasized ecosystem conservation, particularly the role of refuges within ecosystems, and their ability to affect the long-term conservation of natural resources. Implementing an ecosystem approach to resource management is one of our top national priorities. We have initiated new partnerships with private landowners, state and federal agencies, corporations, conservation groups, and volunteers, to form 52 ecosystem teams across the country, typically using large river watersheds to define ecosystems. Those teams work on developing goals and priorities for research and management within each ecosystem.

The Refuge Complex lies within our Connecticut River/Long Island Sound Ecosystem (Map 1-3). A team composed of Fish and Wildlife Service personnel and representatives from six State Fish and Wildlife Departments developed a Priority Resources Plan (July 1996) that identifies seven priorities, each involving numerous action strategies.

1. Protect, restore, and enhance listed and candidate populations...with special emphasis on beach strand species, coastal sandplain habitat, and Connecticut River species.

2. Protect, restore, and enhance anadromous and interjurisdictional migratory fish populations...with special emphasis on Atlantic salmon, American shad, shortnose sturgeon, and river herring.

3. Reverse the decline of migrant landbirds...with special emphasis on grassland and forest interior species.

4. Protect, restore, and enhance populations of colonial nesting waterbirds, shorebirds, and waterfowl...with special emphasis on coastal areas and major rivers.

5. Protect, restore, and enhance wetland habitats.

Map 1-3

Connecticut River/Long Island Sound Ecosystem
Rhode Island NWR Complex Comprehensive Conservation Plan

CANADA

ME

VT

NH

NY

MA

CT

RI

ATLANTIC OCEAN

6. Manage refuge lands to protect, restore, and enhance native communities and trust resources.

7. Develop a public that values the fish and wildlife resources...understands events and issues related to these resources, and acts to promote fish and wildlife conservation.

Regional Wetlands Concept Plan – Emergency Wetlands Resources Act 9 (USFWS 1990)

In 1986, Congress enacted the Emergency Wetlands Resources Act to promote the conservation of our nation's wetlands. The Act directed the Department of Interior to develop a National Wetlands Priority Conservation Plan identifying the location and types of wetlands that should receive priority for acquisition by federal and state agencies using Land and Water Conservation Fund appropriations. In 1990, the Service's Northeast Region completed a Regional Wetlands Concept Plan identifying a total of 850 wetland sites in the Region warranting consideration for acquisition due to wetland values. Wetland values, functions, and potential threats for each site were cited; 24 sites within the State of Rhode Island were listed.

Protecting Our Land Resources:
A Land Acquisition and Protection Plan, Rhode Island Department of Environmental Management, May 1996

The purpose of this State plan is to assist agencies within the Rhode Island Department of Environmental Management (RI DEM) in protecting land to support their primary mission, "...protection of the integrity of natural resources essential to the environmental, economic and social welfare of the citizens of Rhode Island." Its framework provides strategies to permanently protect five critical State resources: agriculture, forestry, drinking water, recreation, and natural heritage and biodiversity. It includes evaluation criteria for selecting and prioritizing lands.

Special Area Management Plan – Narrow River, November 1998

This plan details management strategies for implementing the program standards of the State of Rhode Island Coastal Resources Management Council (CRMC) in the Narrow River Watershed. The Narrow River SAMP defines these objectives relevant to our CCP:

1. Provide for a balance of compatible uses, consistent with the CRMC responsibility for preserving, protecting, and restoring coastal resources.

2. Provide a regional plan for the Narrow River that recognizes that the watershed functions as an ecosystem.

3. Identify ways nitrogen can be reduced in the watershed through new technologies.

4. Revise and update existing policies and standards as well as recommendations to municipalities and federal and state agencies.

5. Update all maps using the Rhode Island Geographic Information System, and modify SAMP boundaries as needed to manage for erosion and water quality pollution.

6. Identify and prioritize future research agendas for the region.

Existing partnerships

Throughout this CCP, we use the term "partners". In addition to our volunteers, we receive significant help from the following partners:

- Southern New England/New York Bight Coastal Ecosystems Office (FWS)
- Ecological Services, New England Field Office (FWS)
- Friends of the National Wildlife Refuges of Rhode Island
- Rhode Island Department of Environmental Management (RI DEM)
- The Nature Conservancy, Rhode Island and Block Island Offices
- University of Rhode Island, Department of Natural Resources Science (URI)
- Audubon Society of Rhode Island
- Rhode Island Coastal Resources Management Council (RI CRMC)
- Local land trusts
- Narragansett Indian Tribal Council

Chapter 2

Public Open House presenting CCP, Rhode Island
USFWS photo

Planning Process

- The Comprehensive Conservation Planning Process
- Issues, Concerns, and Opportunities

The Comprehensive Conservation Planning Process

Given the mandate in the Refuge Improvement Act to develop a CCP for each national wildlife refuge, our Northeast Regional Office identified nine refuges for initial planning during 1998 and 1999. We began the planning process for the Refuge Complex when its planning team of Regional Office and Refuge Complex staff first convened in February 1998. Figure 2-1 displays the steps of the planning process and how they incorporate NEPA requirements.

First, we focused on collecting information on natural resources and public use at the Refuge Complex, and developed its long-term vision and preliminary goals, including issues associated with each of its refuges. Next, we compiled a mailing list of more than 2,000 organizations and individuals, to ensure we would be contacting a diverse sample of the interested public.

Recognizing that not everyone could attend the Open Houses planned for April and May 1998, we developed Issues Workbooks in March, to encourage even more people to provide their written comments on topics related to managing the Refuge Complex. We offered the workbooks to everyone on our mailing list, including adjacent landowners, and made workbooks available at refuge headquarters, local libraries, and on the Internet from the Region 5 home page (http://www.northeast.fws.gov). We received 150 completed workbooks. Those responses and public input at our meetings have influenced our formulating issues and developing alternatives on resource protection and public use.

Figure 2-1. *National Environmental Policy Act (NEPA) and the CCP Process*

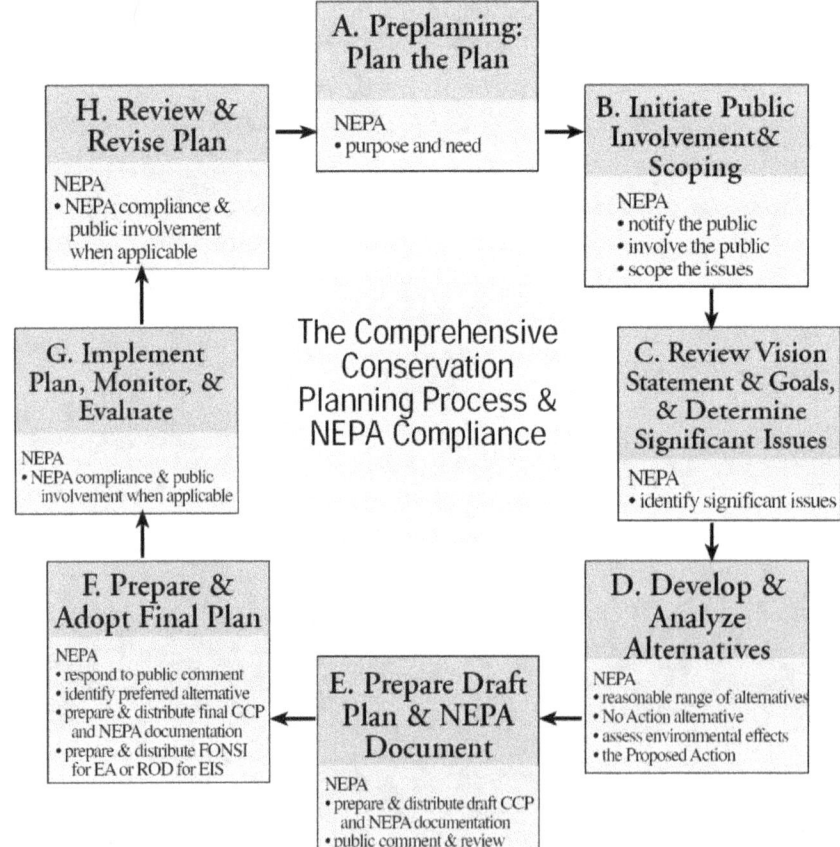

In April and May 1998, we began a series of public meetings: five Open Houses in the communities of Middletown, South Kingstown, Charlestown, and Block Island invited public comments on goals and issues. We advertised the meetings through news releases, radio broadcasts, and notices to our mailing list. From 15 to 40 people attended each meeting. We also organized 15 informational meetings with state and federal agencies, non-profit conservation groups, town planners, conservation commissions, and sporting clubs.

Public responses suggested more than 50 additional areas where lands warranted protection, typically along the coast. We evaluated those lands for their potential as national wildlife refuges, using criteria such as the presence of threatened, endangered, or other trust species and their habitats, the presence of wetlands, our ability to manage or restore the areas, existing threats to their integrity, and their size and location.

We distributed a Planning Update to everyone on our mailing list in September 1998. This newsletter summarized public comments from meetings and workbooks, described policy guidelines for managing public use on refuges, and identified the long-term vision and goals for the Refuge Complex.

Once the key issues had firmed up, we developed alternative strategies by May 1999 to resolve each one. We derived the strategies from public comment, from follow-up contacts with partners, or from the planning team. We distributed a second Planning Update newsletter in May 1999, updating everyone on our planning timelines and our decision to start a separate Environmental Assessment for the visitor center/headquarters.

We released a draft CCP/EA in December of 2000 for a 51-day comment period. We held public hearings and open houses in February of 2001. A summary of public comments and our response to them is included in Appendix B. The land acquisition component of the process is in the Land Protection Plan, Appendix E.

Each year, we will evaluate our accomplishments under this CCP, including the completion of more detailed step down plans. Monitoring or new information results may indicate the need to change our strategies. We will modify the CCP documents and associated management activities as needed, following the procedures outlined in Service policy and NEPA requirements. This CCP will be fully revised every 15 years, or sooner if necessary.

Issues, Concerns, and Opportunities

From the Issues Workbooks, public and focus group meetings, and planning team discussions, we developed for each refuge a list of issues, concerns, opportunities, or any other items requiring a management decision. Then we sorted them into two categories: "Key issues," and "Issues and concerns considered outside the scope of this analysis".

Key issues, along with the goals, formed the basis for developing and comparing the draft CCP/EA alternatives. Issues outside the scope of our analysis were described in the draft CCP/EA, but will not be addressed further in this final CCP.

Key Issues

Public and partner meetings and further team discussions produced the key issues briefly described below.

1. Protection of endangered and threatened species and other species and habitats of special concern.

This is the most important issue facing the refuge. Protecting federally listed endangered and threatened species is integral to the mission of the Refuge System. Other federal trust species are also of primary concern, including migratory birds, anadromous fish, and certain marine mammals.

Appendix A lists species and habitats of special management concern. The list includes the status of all plants, wildlife, fish, and rare natural communities known to occur in Rhode Island that are federally listed as endangered or threatened, were candidates for listing, or are otherwise of management concern. Combined with location information, we used that list to identify additional land protection needs and opportunities. We know very little about many of these species' presence on or use of refuge habitats. The alternatives in the draft CCP/EA differed in their strategies for managing these species and habitats. Addressing this issue will help achieve Goal 1: Protect and enhance federal trust resources and other species and habitats of special concern.

2. Restoration and maintenance of coastal sandplain natural communities, including grasslands and shrublands (less than 60 years old).

While it is true that the Northeast landscape was primarily forested prior to rapid agricultural settlement in the 1800's, grasslands quickly became a dominant part of the landscape in the 19th century. Grassland-dependent species responded in kind and became established. Over the last several decades, however, coastal sandplain grasslands and shrublands, coastal maritime grasslands and shrublands, and agricultural fields and pastures, have been in rapid decline in New England due to a combination of development, changes in agricultural technology, succession to forest as farms were abandoned, and lack of a natural disturbance such as fire (Vickery 1997).

In Rhode Island, the State's farmland dropped nearly 50 percent between 1964 and 1997, from 103,801 to 55,256 acres. An additional 3,100 acres of farmland will be lost in the next 20 years if current sprawl patterns continue (Common Ground 2000). As a result, few large, contiguous grasslands and shrublands are left; only smaller, fragmented, and isolated habitat patches remain (<75 acres).

These smaller areas are unsuitable for many focus species, including once-common grassland birds such as grasshopper sparrow and upland sandpiper. Grasshopper sparrows have declined by 69 percent in the past 25 years, according to Breeding Bird Survey data (Vickery 1997). Our best available information suggests that grasslands should ideally be managed in 100 acre or larger patches. Smaller grassland habitat patches are much less productive for grassland birds, and could serve as "sinks", where species try to nest, but becaused of increased predation and other factors, productivity and survival is severely limited.

Other grassland and shrubland species have declined dramatically as well. Many of Rhode Island's State-listed plant and animal species are dependent on these habitat types.

Tremendous potential exists for refuge staff to become involved in restoring habitat on private lands. Grassland and shrubland restoration offers opportunities for our staff to provide technical expertise to local communities. The alternatives in the draft CCP/EA compared different levels of restoring and maintaining these habitats and providing technical assistance to private landowners. Addressing this issue will help achieve Goal 2: Maintain and/or restore natural ecological communities to promote healthy, functioning ecosystems.

3. Protection and restoration of wetlands.

The well documented values of healthy wetlands include fish and wildlife habitat, flood protection, erosion control, and water quality maintenance. Despite laws and regulations to protect them, wetlands throughout Rhode Island have been rapidly declining since the 1960's through conversion to agriculture, residential and industrial development. Rhode Island has developed more land in the last 34 years than in its first 325 years (Common Ground May/June 2000). Most recent sprawl occurs outside the urban areas, near the remaining wetlands.

Estuarine wetlands consisting of tidal salt and brackish waters are of particular concern. Invasive species are dominating refuge wetlands and threatening their biodiversity.

Non-point pollution and sources off-refuge are impacting water quality and the health and productivity of these wetlands. The alternatives in the draft CCP/EA compared different levels of management for restoring wetlands and for cooperatively managing entire watersheds. Addressing this issue will help achieve Goal 2: Maintain and/or restore natural ecological communities to promote healthy, functioning ecosystems.

4. Maintenance of water quality in the Narrow River.

The Narrow River provides many values beneficial to a diverse array of wildlife and to the surrounding communities. Many wildlife species use the estuary and adjacent wetlands as a primary food source, a migratory rest stop, and as breeding, nesting, and spawning grounds.

The quality of both groundwater and surface water continues to deteriorate as a result of residential and commercial development within the watershed and the associated contribution of non-point pollutants such as individual septic systems. Since 1959, the Narrow River has failed to meet State standards for coliform bacteria, and parts of the river have been closed to shell fishing since 1979. Its degraded water quality threatens wetland habitats in Chafee Refuge, constraining their ability to fulfill the refuge purpose. The alternatives in the draft CCP/EA evaluated different levels of involvement in cooperatively managing and protecting the watershed. Addressing this issue will help achieve Goal 2: Maintain and/or restore natural ecological communities to promote healthy, functioning ecosystems.

5. Control of invasive, non-native, or overabundant plant and wildlife species.

Each of the five refuges has an extensive distribution of invasive plant species. These plants are a threat because they displace native plant and animal species, degrade wetlands and other natural communities, and reduce natural diversity and wildlife habitat values. They outcompete native species by dominating light, water, and nutrient resources. Once established, getting rid of invasive plants is expensive and labor-intensive. Unfortunately, their characteristic abilities to establish easily, reproduce prolifically, and disperse readily, make eradication difficult.

Many of these plants cause measurable economic impacts, particularly in agricultural fields. Preventing new invasions is extremely important for maintaining biodiversity and native plant populations. The control of existing, affected areas will require extensive partnerships with adjacent landowners, state, and local governments.

Thirteen invasive plant species affecting the natural communities within the Refuge Complex are considered of high management concern. The most prevalent are *Phragmites*, purple loosestrife, Asian bittersweet, autumn olive, and Japanese honeysuckle. Other species such as Japanese knotweed and multiflora rose are increasing on the Refuge Complex, and likely to become an issue soon.

Several wildlife species occur on the Refuge Complex that are known, or suspected to be, adversely affecting natural diversity. Issues surface when these species directly impact federal trust species or degrade natural communities. Mute swans are non-native, invasive species that aggressively drive native waterfowl and shorebirds away from nesting areas, compete with them for food, degrade water quality when they spend extended periods of time molting on coastal ponds, and are sometimes aggressive towards humans.

Native species such as deer, red fox, gull, and small predatory mammals such as mink, skunk, and weasel can be a problem when their populations exceed the range of natural fluctuation and the ability of the habitat to support them. Excessive numbers of deer are a threat to rare plant communities on the Refuge Complex, and excessive browse lines are evident on two refuges. Adjacent landowners are also concerned about deer impacts on landscaping, the increase in vehicle-deer collisions, and the threat of Lyme disease.

Red fox, gull, and some small mammals are voracious predators that can adversely impact other native wildlife populations. Occurrences have been documented of herring and black-backed gull, red fox, and weasel preying on piping plover and least tern, a State-listed species (threatened). Fox easily habituate to humans, and were being hand-fed at Sachuest Point Refuge. Many people fear fox and other mammals because they can carry rabies. These predators are particularly troublesome when their populations exceed natural levels. Control measures for each species are controversial, and may include lethal removal, visual and audio deterrents, or destroying eggs, nests, or den sites.

The alternatives in the draft CCP/EA compared different strategies for managing invasive species. Addressing this issue will help achieve Goal 1: Protect and enhance Federal trust resources and other species and habitats of special concern, and Goal 2: Maintain and/or restore natural ecological communities to promote healthy, functioning ecosystems.

6. Protection of biologically significant areas through acquisition and/or cooperative management.

Public meetings, partner meetings, and workbook responses expressed a great deal of support for the protection of additional fish and wildlife habitat in southern Rhode Island. That support runs across the State, as Rhode Islanders consistently vote ballot measures to maintain open space and protect fish and wildlife habitats. Many people mentioned that their support stems from their concern over the rapid pace of development on the South Shore. As we stated earlier, development in non-urban areas of Rhode Island has increased dramatically over the last 30 years. It is now the second most densely populated State in the country. One estimate predicts that current sprawl patterns will ensure the loss of all its rural areas before 2100 (Common Ground 2000). The Rhode Island office of The Nature Conservancy has noted that the conservation actions taken during the next 5 to 10 years will be the most important for the majority of Rhode Island towns (The Nature Conservancy 2000).

This dramatic increase in development has changed land use patterns and practices, significantly modifying natural landscapes. As natural lands (those with sustainable native species populations and intact ecological processes) become isolated and fragmented into smaller pieces disconnected from other natural areas, their ability to support a full complement of native species is adversely affected. Cut off from larger populations, species and plant communities within these natural areas face the problems of limited genetic exchange, a decreased ability to support diverse populations, and lost capacity to recruit new individuals. Ultimately, the number of native species declines and exotic species gain a stronghold. It is precisely this diminished ability of natural areas to support diverse species with different habitat requirements that leads to a decline in biodiversity. While some species can tolerate fragmentation as they prefer "edge habitat," many others, including "interior" dependent species, require larger, contiguous natural areas or functional corridors linking patches of natural habitat. This ability to protect and sustain larger natural areas and corridors, coupled with the protection of unique or rare species or communities, is critical to maintaining biodiversity.

A landscape or ecosystem approach to protecting land is also critical in the recovery of threatened and endangered species. Piping plover serve to illustrate this point. They have a fairly strong fidelity to certain nesting areas and typically return to them most years. Shifting of pairs between nesting areas has been observed when disturbances or habitat conditions affect their ability to nest. Barrier beaches are dynamic ecosystems, and their nesting conditions can change dramatically from year to year. While 1999 was a good nesting year on Moonstone Beach (Trustom Pond Refuge), in 2000, the beach consisted entirely of cobble with virtually no sand for nesting. The piping plover pairs from 1999 appeared to have shifted to the Ninigret Conservation Area. Without consideration of these shifts in habitat use across a landscape, management for these species would be ineffective.

Some individuals preferred that the Service acquire and manage federal trust resources, and that the Refuge Complex continue to acquire these sites. Others emphasized partnerships to cooperatively protect and manage important habitats not currently on refuge land. Still others recommended a combination of Service acquisition and cooperative management to provide the greatest long-term benefit to resources. At public meetings and in our workbooks, many responses suggested specific areas needing protection, particularly wetlands threatened by development. Some individuals we spoke with especially supported our acquiring land occupied by endangered or threatened species.

The alternatives in the draft CCP/EA offered various levels of Service land acquisition, ranging from lands within the currently approved acquisition boundaries only, to a considerable expansion of each refuge's acquisition boundary. They also evaluated our increased involvement in cooperative land protection off-refuge. Addressing this issue will help achieve Goal 3: Establish a land protection program that fully supports accomplishment of species, habitat, and ecosystem goals.

7. Assurance of access to credible information about resources regarding the Refuge Complex to ensure management decisions are based on the best available science.

We need to determine and prioritize what information reasonably could be collected to facilitate decision-making using the best available science. In particular, many individuals expressed concern over the lack of information available to fully evaluate impacts to wildlife and habitats from excessive public use. Others questioned the effectiveness of management actions that have not been adequately monitored and evaluated. Several university researchers and other partners encouraged our staff to prioritize baseline inventory needs, establish monitoring protocols to better evaluate management actions, and identify information needed to determine each refuge's contribution to the ecosystem.

Implementing the Service's *Policy on Maintaining the Biological Integrity, Diversity, and Environmental Health of the National Wildlife Refuge System* will require us to ascertain the natural conditions for each refuge and identify the natural communities, species, and ecological processes that are rare, declining, or unique. Opportunities to cooperate in collecting this information could be developed once the priorities have been identified. The alternatives in the draft CCP/EA offered different levels of pursuing this information. Addressing this issue will help achieve all the Goals identified for the Refuge Complex.

8. Management of public use and access.

The Refuge Improvement Act and Service policy require our enhanced consideration of opportunities for six priority wildlife-dependent uses (see above). Some level of each occurs on the Refuge Complex. Only those uses that are compatible with a refuge's purpose may be allowed. According to Service policy, all refuges are closed to any use until it is formally opened through the compatibility determination process.

The act also directs refuges to terminate immediately or phase out as expeditiously as practicable, existing uses determined to be not compatible. Non-wildlife-dependent uses exist on all the refuges, and some have been occurring for years. Examples include jogging, sunbathing and swimming, bicycling, and dog walking.
Input from public meetings and workbook responses make it clear that public use on refuges is extremely important to most people. More than 90 percent ranked environmental education and interpretation and wildlife observation and photography very high as desirable public uses. Rarely, however, was there consensus on other public uses or just how much of each type to allow. Public opinion

spans the entire spectrum from those wanting to open up refuges to non-wildlife-dependent activities, to those who want to close refuges to all public use to maintain an undisturbed sanctuary for wildlife.

The alternatives in the draft CCP/EA compared different levels and combinations of wildlife-dependent public use. Addressing this issue will help achieve Goal 4: Provide opportunities for high quality, compatible, wildlife-dependent public use with particular emphasis on environmental education and interpretation.

9. Hunting.

Hunting surfaced late in the scoping process as a key issue, perhaps because, initially, few viewed it as a possibility on the Refuge Complex. This issue was raised by Service personnel, by RI DEM biologists, and by individuals both for and against expanding hunting opportunities on the Refuge Complex. Those in support primarily are interested in deer hunting on all refuges, waterfowl hunting on Chafee Refuge and Ninigret Refuge, and pheasant hunting on Block Island. Advocates of hunting refer to its inclusion as one of the six priority public uses that "...shall receive priority consideration in refuge planning and management" (1997 Refuge Improvement Act).

The Service views managed or administrative hunts in areas where there are overabundant deer populations as an effective tool for regulating them. Responses generally agree that the overabundance of deer is a concern in Rhode Island, reflected in increased numbers of vehicle-deer collisions, increased complaints about deer browsing on commercial and residential landscape plantings, visible impacts on native vegetation, and higher concern about contracting Lyme disease.

Those opposed to hunting cited concerns with public safety, disturbance and harm to other wildlife species, and the impact to visitors engaged in the other five priority public uses. The latter results from the likelihood that significant portions of the refuges, due to their small sizes and configurations, would be closed to other activities during hunting. Some expressed the opinion that the refuges should function as a sanctuary for all native species, and that hunting is incongruous with that function.

The alternatives in the draft CCP/EA offered varying levels of hunting opportunities, from no hunting at all, to opening four refuges during State-regulated seasons for deer, waterfowl, and pheasant. Addressing this issue will help achieve both Goal 2: Maintain and/or restore natural ecological communities to promote healthy, functioning ecosystems, and Goal 4: Provide opportunities for high quality, compatible, wildlife-dependent public use with particular emphasis on environmental education and interpretation.

10. Opportunities for environmental education.

Responses so frequently mentioned increasing environmental educational opportunities across the Refuge Complex that our planning team decided it warranted special recognition. More than 90 percent of the workbook responses ranked environmental education and interpretation as one of their top three interests. The alternatives in the draft CCP/EA compared different levels of environmental educational opportunities and the different levels of partnerships so integral to implementing them on each of the five refuges. Addressing this issue will help achieve Goal 4: Provide opportunities for high quality, compatible, wildlife-dependent public use with particular emphasis on environmental education and interpretation.

11. Provision of staffing, operations, and maintenance support sufficient to accomplish goals and objectives.

The Refuge Complex lacks adequate funding and personnel to provide the programs and services desired by the public and to effectively meet the goals for this CCP. The alternatives in the draft CCP/EA compared different funding and staffing levels based on their proposed management strategies for dealing with the issues. Addressing this issue will help achieve Goal 5: Provide Refuge Complex staffing, operations, and maintenance support to effectively accomplish refuge goals and objectives.

12. Increasing the visibility of the Fish and Wildlife Service.

Our lack of visibility on refuges was brought up repeatedly at public meetings and in the workbooks. Many people felt strongly about the need for more refuge staff to be present during peak visitation to increase resource protection and improve visitor services. Other recommendations to increase visibility included more visitor contact stations, increasing wildlife interpretation and environmental educational opportunities, a better location for a headquarters office, developing a Refuge Complex visitor center, improving existing visitor facilities (e.g., kiosks, interpretive signs on trails, etc.), increasing support for a volunteer program, and increasing community involvement.

Some people expressed an interest in seeing refuge staff enforce public use policy more consistently. Others argued it was unnecessary for Service personnel to be armed while patrolling beaches. The alternatives in the draft CCP/EA compared different levels of promoting our visibility and providing these services. Addressing this issue will help achieve both Goal 2: Maintain and/or restore natural ecological communities to promote healthy, functioning ecosystems, and Goal 4: Provide opportunities for high quality, compatible, wildlife-dependent public use with particular emphasis on environmental education and interpretation.

13. Need for improved facilities.

The Refuge Complex lacks a facilities plan establishing current and future needs for staff operations and visitor services. Many of its current facilities are inadequate. Its headquarters does not have enough office space to accommodate even current staff, and the visitor services area is limited to one rack of literature in the reception area. The alternatives in the draft CCP/EA compared opportunities for new or improved facilities to accommodate staff work space, increase the visibility of the Service and the Refuge Complex, and improve visitor services, including environmental education and interpretation. Addressing this issue will help achieve Goal 5: Provide Refuge Complex staffing, operations, and maintenance support to effectively accomplish refuge goals and objectives.

Chapter 3

Piping plover
USFWS photo

Refuge and Resource Descriptions

- Geographic/Ecosystem Setting
- Socioeconomic Setting
- Refuge Complex Administration
- Refuge Resources
- Cultural Resources
- Public Uses

Geographic/Ecosystem Setting

Landscape Formation

The movement of glaciers across New England created the land forms seen in Rhode Island today. The last of those great ice sheets occurred during the Wisconsin glacial period. Approximately 15,000 - 20,000 years ago, the glacier was in a state of equilibrium, where the melting rate of ice equaled the glacial rate of movement (Bell 1985). As the climate warmed 12,000 - 15,000 years ago, the glacier began its retreat, depositing pronounced land forms along its outermost edge. The southern coast of Rhode Island, including Block Island, is the farthest point the Wisconsin glacier reached in its southeastern frontal movement. The retreating glacier deposited rocks pushed by the front of its ice sheet in piles called moraines. These terminal or end moraines formed sinuous ridges up to 200 feet high. Block Island is part of the terminal moraine that includes Nantucket and parts of Long Island.

A second prominent moraine lies inland, the low ridge referred to as the Charlestown or Watch Hill moraine, stretching east to west parallel to U.S. Route 1. Glacial action also created other features in today's landscape: recessional moraines, outwash plains, kettle hole ponds, glacial lake deposits, deltas, and submerged gravel shoals. Prominent headlands like Sachuest Point are composed of glacial till, a mixture of silt-sized grains to boulder-sized deposits by the melting glacier.

Melting ice sheets caused the sea to rise rapidly across Block Island and Rhode Island Sounds until it reached its present level approximately 4,000 years ago. Wave action parallel to the shore continued to erode glacial deposits, creating the barrier spits. As the spits formed, they almost entirely sealed off the low-lying areas between the headlands and the ocean, forming coastal lagoons connected to the sea by narrow inlets. These became the coastal salt ponds we see today. Through the 1700's, all of the coastal salt ponds had direct, seasonally open connections to the ocean (RI CRMC 1984). The effects of erosion through time have shifted the salt ponds and barrier spits gradually landward (RI CRMC 1998).

The bedrock formations of southern Rhode Island include the Blackstone series of metamorphic rock along its southern coastal border (including most of Westerly, Charlestown and South Kingstown), granite rock of various ages (including most of Narragansett and Middletown and parts of Westerly and Charlestown), and Pennsylvanian sedimentary rock in most of south central Rhode Island (including Richmond, much of South Kingstown, and most of Hopkinton). Most of the soils around the refuges are fine sandy loams or silt loams.

Historical Influences on Landscape Vegetation

The upland forests of southern Rhode Island are classified by Kuchler (1964) as oak-hickory forest; while most of northern Rhode Island is classified as oak-pitch pine forest. Historic land use practices promoted this forest type.

As early as 12,000 years ago, Native Americans began occupying the area. Documented evidence places the first intensive occupation of the salt pond region during the late Archaic period (5,000 to 3,000 years ago). Native American camps from more than 4,000 years ago are known to have existed at one location along the shore of Ninigret Pond. However, societies of that time were primarily hunter-gatherer with little agriculture; broad changes to landscape vegetation probably did not occur.

During the Woodland Period 3000-450 years ago, larger, semi-permanent or recurrently occupied camps became coastal settlements. Fortified villages are known to have existed in some locations. Maize horticulture became prominent, which likely resulted in small clearings. Larger clearings and burnings to control the movement of deer and upland birds may have occurred, and the first pronounced clearing of land along the coast for settlements, game management, and agriculture. Much of this land was cleared by cutting and burning, which favored resprouting by hardwood species like oak, hickory, and red maple.

The role fire may have played in shaping landscape vegetation is not well known. Evidence of fire has been observed in charcoal layers at Ninigret Refuge. Soil cores dug at most points on the refuge reveal charcoal below the historic farmers plow zone, approximately 10 inches soil depth. The dates attributed to these fires, coupled with their locations, suggest early Native Americans used fire extensively and purposefully.

Although small areas of land were cleared and more or less permanently settled by early Native Americans, it was European settlement and expansion in the 1600's that exponentially escalated the conversion of forests to agriculture. The eighteenth century Rhode Island plantation era "...required massive land clearing of the forests that had dominated the landscapes for the last 8,000 years" (USFWS 1999). During the mid-nineteenth century, an estimated 85 percent of southern New England was converted to field and pasture. Any woods remaining often were managed for firewood (Jorgensen 1977).

A detailed report on the archeological history of the Refuge Complex is available from the Refuge Complex office on request (Jacobson USFWS).

Contemporary Influences on the Landscape

The major natural disturbances affecting the coastline today are hurricanes and winter ice-storms. Hurricanes have the greatest impact, by far. The straight border of barrier beaches separated from the mainland by tidal wetlands and coastal salt ponds characterizes a coastline influenced by frequent storms. Wind and waves pick up loose sand and sediment and move it along the shoreline or back out to sea, allowing occasional overwash of barrier beaches and breaching of coastal ponds. Overwash, tidal currents, longshore currents, and rip currents are all mechanisms transporting sediment along the barrier beaches (RI CRMC 1998).

Fall and winter storms combining wind, rain, and waves are the predominant physical process shaping this landscape today. "Nor'easters" are well known along the New England coast in winter, winds generated offshore from the southeast, can actually be more destructive to the south shore, because of its exposure to the open ocean. The draft Salt Pond Region Special Area Management Plan describes the geologic, wave, and wind action for the South Shore, including details on how sediment movement constantly reshapes this dynamic landscape (RI CRMC 1998).

The Great New England Hurricane of 1938 was the most recent 100-year storm, one of immense power along the coast. Not only did winds reach speeds up to 240 miles per hour, but also a spring high tide created a storm surge between 10 and 15 feet. Storms of this magnitude are suspected to have occurred only four other times in recorded history: 1635, 1683, 1815, and 1821 (Bell 1985). Smaller hurricanes are less powerful but more frequent than the hurricane of 1938. Hurricanes in 1944, 1954, 1955, 1960, 1976, and Hurricane Bob in 1991 each left its mark on the coastline.

Human influences on sustaining the form and function of coastal landscapes and ecosystems over the long term are predominantly negative. Attempts to stabilize the beach system by constructing jetties or breach ways and planting beach grass have greatly affected the natural dynamics of this system by interrupting the natural flow of waves and sediment. In fact, the breach ways connecting the ponds to the ocean and one pond to another are the single greatest human impact on the ecology of coastal ponds (RI CRMC 1984).

Introducing non-native, invasive plants, diverting or draining coastal wetlands for development, converting uplands for residential use, and spilling oil are other significant human impacts on the coastal landscape. Recent studies indicate that the greatest threats to Rhode Island's estuaries and coastal salt ponds are septic systems and road runoff (RI DEM 1996). More studies are needed to establish the extent to which each of these factors influences Refuge Complex ecosystems.

On Rhode Island's upland landscape, a combination of management and natural succession has allowed forests to make a comeback. The State Division of Forest Environment estimates that 300,000 acres of privately owned forest plus 45,000 acres of State-managed forest make up 45 percent of the State's land area. Their estimate places 80 percent of the privately owned forest in tracts from 1 to 10 acres in size, which are difficult to manage as forest and are rapidly being converted to residential areas (RI DEM 1996).

Ecosystem Delineations

The Service emphasizes an ecosystem approach to conservation, typically using large river watersheds to define ecosystems. Rhode Island falls within our Connecticut River/Long Island Sound Ecosystem (map 1-3).

Another commonly used delineation of ecosystems was developed by Bailey (USDA 1978, expanded 1995). These ecologically based map units often are used in landscape-level analyses. An ecoregion is first divided into a domain, then a division, a province, a section, and a subsection. Each level defines in greater detail its geomorphology, geology, soil, climate, potential vegetation, surface water, and current human use. Each of these resource attributes has implications for resource management. For example, opportunities to restore native grasslands may be limited by soil types, potential vegetation, and the extent of human impacts on the natural environment. Rhode Island falls within the Humid Temperate Domain, Hot Continental Division, Eastern Broadleaf Forest Province, and Lower New England Section.

Climate

Cold winters and warm summers with a moderating ocean influence characterize Rhode Island's climate. Winter temperatures average 30° F, with lowest temperatures ranging between -10° F and -20° F. Summer temperatures average 70° F, and peak in the 90s. Annual precipitation averages 44 to 48 inches, evenly distributed throughout the year. Thunderstorms occur throughout the summer (USFWS 1989).

Air Quality

The Clean Air Act establishes Class I, II, and III areas with limits on the amount of "criteria air pollutants" that can exist in pre-defined geographic areas. Examples of criteria air pollutants are smog (primarily ground-level ozone), particulate matter, and carbon monoxide. Class I areas allow very little additional deterioration of air quality (e.g. Wilderness Areas); Class II areas allow for more deterioration; and Class III areas allow even more. All of Rhode Island is currently classified as a Class II area. The U.S. Environmental Protection Agency (EPA) has designated the entire State a serious non-attainment area for ozone. That designation resulted in stricter automobile emissions standards designed to reduce emissions by 24 percent between 1990 and 1999.

Socio-economic Factors

The Refuge Complex lies close to some of the largest population centers on the east coast. The New York City metropolitan area, population 8.5 million, is 2.5 hours to the southeast. Metropolitan Boston, population 3.2 million, is 2 hours to the north. Hartford, with a population of 140,000, is 1.5 hours to the northwest, and Providence, population 161,000, is 45 minutes to the north (U.S. Census Bureau 1996 estimates and 1990 U.S. Census).

According to those estimates, the population of Rhode Island is about 1 million; 94 percent live in metropolitan areas (cf. the national average of 80 percent) and 6 percent in rural areas. South County, which includes Ninigret Refuge , Trustom Pond Refuge , and Chafee Refuge , has the fastest growing population and the highest number of building permits issued annually (RI CRMC 1998). South County population figures between 1990 and 1996 increased 7.4 percent, 4.6 percent, and 5.3 percent respectively in Charlestown, Narragansett, and South Kingstown, while Middletown's population decreased by 1.4 percent. The Town of New Shoreham, which includes Block Island, had a population increase of 10.8 percent. The population for the entire state of Rhode Island decreased by 1.3 percent over the same period (http://www.riedc.com).

The Refuge Complex directly contributes to the economies of Charlestown, South Kingstown, Narragansett, Middletown, and New Shoreham through refuge revenue sharing payments. The Federal Government does not pay property tax; it does pay refuge revenue sharing directly to cities and towns each year, based on the fair market value of refuge lands. The revenue sharing formula calculates three-quarters of 1 percent of the fair market value of refuge lands as the maximum amount payable each year. An appraisal updated every five years keeps their fair market value current. The actual amount of revenue sharing paid each year varies, depending on what portion of the maximum amount Congress appropriates that year (rarely the maximum). Figure 3-1 depicts refuge revenue sharing payments to those towns for the fiscal year 2000.

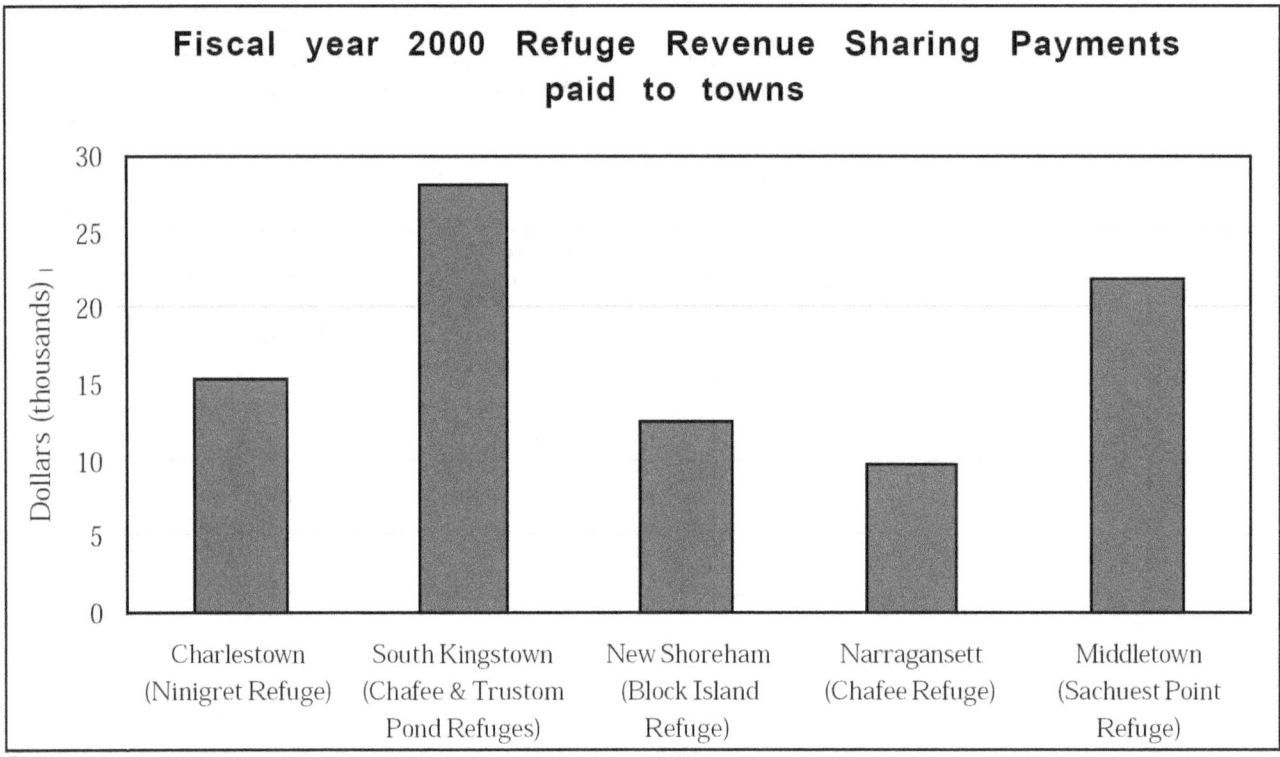

Figure 3-1. *Refuge Revenue Sharing Payments made to towns in 2000.*

The University of Rhode Island Department of Resource Economics (Spring 1997) reports that travel and tourism is the State's fastest growing industry. In 1996, it generated $1.7 billion. The number of visitors to the State in 1997 increased at a rate twice the national average. Also in 1997, Rhode Island's services industry, which includes those in health, business, and education, comprised the largest wage and salary employment at 34 percent (RI EDC 1997). Between 1987 and 1997, the services industry increased by 37 percent, while the manufacturing industry decreased by 37 percent.

In all the communities surrounding the refuges, travel and tourism and the services that support them contribute substantially to local economies. According to Ann O'Neill, President of the South County Tourism Council (O'Neill 1999), the tourist season lasts from April through October, with peak activity during the summer months. Responses to our workbooks confirm that beaches and water-associated recreation are the primary attractions for visitors with destinations along the Rhode Island coast.

Current travel and tourism literature does not feature the Refuge Complex. According to Ms. O'Neill, its refuges are not well known as tourist destinations, although many visitors discover them during their visit and enjoy the scenery and open space they provide. They are small enough to explore in one day, and generally do not prompt an additional night's lodging. Ms. O'Neill stated that, since the Tourism Council is trying to showcase a greater mix of outdoor recreational opportunities in South County, the Refuge Complex will figure more prominently in future promotional material.

The greatest contribution by the Refuge Complex to the local economy comes from the values attributed to the preservation of open space (NPS 1992). We represent those values using three indicators, below: Cost of Community Services; Property Values; and Public Willingness to Pay.

Cost of Community Services compares the cost per dollar of revenue generated by residential or commercial development to that of revenue generated by an open space designation. On the one hand, residential development expands the tax base, but the costs of increased infrastructure and public services (schools, utilities, emergency services, etc.) often offset any increase in revenue. On the other hand, undeveloped land requires few town services and places little pressure on the local infrastructure. The cost per dollar of revenue generated by commercial land typically falls between those of residential and open space.

The American Farmland Trust (1989, 1992, and 1993) and the Commonwealth Research Group (1995) evaluated community revenues and expenses associated with open space vs. residential and commercial development. All available information on the New England States shows that open space and commercial development produced more revenues than costs, while the opposite was true for residential land.

Conversations with local realtors and appraisers helped us evaluate the refuges' influence on property values. Two South County realtors and one realtor/appraiser confirmed that properties adjacent to refuges generally are valued higher (Gross, et al. 1998). That value is realized through increased sales price/acre in properties adjacent to a refuge, compared to otherwise similar properties, and by how quickly those properties sell. Properties with views protected by their proximity to a refuge exhibit an even greater difference. All the realtors estimated, but none with any certainty, that properties adjacent to refuges may realize from 1- to 4-percent increases in property value. All the realtors we spoke with use a property's adjacency to a refuge as an important advertising asset.

Public Willingness to Pay is a method for estimating the monetary value of ecosystem goods and services by determining how much the public would be willing to pay, either in taxes, fees, or opportunity costs, to preserve ecosystem values. In Rhode Island, where coastal ecosystems are threatened by development-at-large, we have used Willingness to Pay to estimate the value of open space preservation.

Rhode Islanders consistently and overwhelmingly vote for bond measures to protect open space. Local and State-wide bond measures passed in 1985, 1986, 1987, and 1989, invested more than $100 million in acquiring land for recreation and open space. A State-wide bond in 1998 passed an additional $15 million specifically for protecting open space (RI CRMC 1998).

Refuge Complex Administration

Staffing and Budget

Table 3-1. *Refuge Complex staffing levels and budgets between 1995 - 1999.*

Fiscal year	Operations	Maintenance	Full time staff	Seasonal staff
1995	$216,299	$85,700	7	3
1996	355,715	23,900	7	3
1997	350,700	97,700	8	4
1998	428,400	171,000	8	4
1999	441,900	28,000	9	2

Annual budget appropriations are highly variable, and commensurately affect our staffing levels. Table 3-1 summarizes budget and staffing levels from 1995 to 1999. Fluctuations reflect funding for special projects, moving costs for new employees, or large equipment purchases. Most of the funding is earmarked; very little discretionary funding is available.

Resource Protection and Visitor Safety

Law enforcement officers, with full authority to enforce federal regulations, are required to ensure resource protection and visitor safety. Three permanent refuge staff have been assigned collateral duties for law enforcement at any time during the course of refuge operations, but those collateral duties draw staff time and resources away from other important programs. We typically hire up to three seasonal staff with law enforcement authority each year.

During the past 5 years, formal notices of violation averaged 15 per year. They typically involved vehicle and pedestrian trespass, vandalism, and waterfowl hunting in closed areas. Well over 100 verbal warnings are also given each year, typically for inadvertently walking or driving in closed areas, littering, walking dogs in a closed area or off-leash, bicycling in closed areas, and digging plants. In 1993, a Trail Warden program began using volunteers to assist in documenting violations. Wardens also inform visitors of public use policy and permitted activities.

Refuge Complex Office

The Refuge Complex office lies in the Shoreline Plaza strip mall in Charlestown. In addition to housing our staff, it also houses our Division of Ecological Services Southern New England/New York Bight Coastal Ecosystem Program five-member staff, an Atlantic Coast Joint Venture staff person, and Friends of the National Wildlife Refuges of Rhode Island.

An environmental assessment was written in 2000, which determined a new location for a Refuge Headquarters and Visitor Center. The new building will be located on Deer Run Road (off Route 1) in Charlestown, RI. The building is currently being designed, with construction to begin in 2003.

Refuge Resources

Physical Resources

Topography and Hydrology

The Narrow River, which forms Pettaquamscutt Cove, has a geologically complex origin. In general, the tidal river and surrounding uplands are remnants of an ancient river valley carved out by glaciation approximately 10,000 years ago. Technically, the Narrow River is an estuary or a lagoon (RI CRMC 1998).

The eastern side of Chafee Refuge slopes sharply down to the Narrow River, with 15-percent (or greater) slopes along Tower Hill Road. Terrain on the eastern side slopes more gradually, averaging 5 to10 percent. In Pettaquamscutt Cove, the relief is low and near sea level. Bedrock is very close to the surface, the soil layer is thin, and depth to the water table is usually less than 3 feet (RI CRMC 1998). The channel between Narragansett Bay and Pettaquamscutt Cove is called "The Narrows."

Narrow River Watershed: A significant source of information on the Narrow River watershed is the Narrow River Special Area Management Plan, Public Review Document (RI CRMC 1998). Water quality in the Narrow River, including Pettaquamscutt Cove, has been a long-standing issue. The University of Rhode Island Watershed Watch program has been conducting at least bi-weekly water quality monitoring since 1992. Three of their monitoring stations (NR-8, NR-9, and NR-10) lie immediately adjacent to the refuge. Water quality has long been a focus issue for the Narrow River Preservation Association. Numerous other water quality studies have been conducted in the Narrow River watershed and are referenced in the Special Area Management Plan.

Beginning in 1959, the Narrow River has failed to meet state standards for total coliform bacteria levels. By 1994, the entire expanse of the Narrow River had been closed to shell fishing (RI CRMC 1998) and remains closed today.

Excessive nitrogen loading is another concern for the Narrow River; however, no State standards for nitrogen exist. Improperly functioning household septic systems are a major, documented source of both nitrogen and bacteria. Nitrogen and bacteria leach into groundwater, potentially affecting both private and public supplies of drinking water. This is significant, since up to 75 percent of the freshwater flowing into the system originates as groundwater (RI CRMC 1998).

Storm water runoff, commercial and residential fertilizer applications, and petroleum hydrocarbons from boating are all implicated in the water quality problems in the Narrow River (RI CRMC 1998). These sources will continue to increase with development in the watershed. At present, 65 percent of the watershed remains undeveloped, but it lies in one of the fastest growing areas of the State. The 35 percent of the watershed that has been developed is primarily residential. Approximately 14 percent of the watershed is designated open space, including the refuge.

Biological Resources

Vegetation

Table 3-2 displays the various cover types dominating Chafee Refuge.

Table 3-2. *Land use/land cover at Chafee Refuge, Washington County, RI. (source: RIGIS)*

Cover-type	Acreage	Percentage
Agricultural	8.2	2.6%
Brushland	6.5	2.0
Developed	7.6	2.4
Forest upland	115.3	36.1
Water	3.7	1.1
Emergent wetland	79.1	24.7
Forest wetland	74.8	23.4
Scrub-scrub wetland	22.8	7.1
Upland	1.8	0.6
Total	**319.8**	**100%**

In the tidal salt marsh portions of the refuge, the dominant vegetation types are salt meadow grass (*Spartina patens*), salt marsh cordgrass (*Spartina alterniflora*), spike grass (*Distichlis spicata*), saltwort (*Salicornia sp.*), and sea lavender (*Limonium nashii*). Several islands in the salt marsh are composed of black oak (*Quercus velutina*), with a poison ivy (*Rhus radicans*) understory. The uplands adjacent to the west side of the river are primarily forested by black oak and red maple, while the uplands on its east side are dominated by red maple. A detailed plant list is available from the Refuge Office upon request (George 1999).

Threatened and Endangered Species

Piping plover, a federally listed species (threatened), and least tern, a State-listed species (threatened), nest at the mouth of the Narrow River, but have a limited presence on the refuge. No other animals that are federal- or State-listed as threatened or endangered are found within the watershed.

The State endangered sea pink plant (*Sabatia stellaris*) is known in the vicinity of the refuge along the Narrow River, but no surveys have been conducted to verify its presence on the refuge.

Birds

Formal surveys will need to be done in the future, especially waterfowl surveys. Although the refuge was established primarily to protect wintering populations of black ducks, we in fact know very little about black duck populations and their use of the refuge. Other waterfowl that commonly winter in the Narrow River watershed are mallards, canvasbacks, bufflehead, mergansers, Canada geese, and the non-native mute swan.

Completion of the North American Waterfowl Management Plan (1986) elevated concern about black ducks. The plan identifies them as a species of "immediate, international concern," and considers the protection of essential migrating and wintering habitats paramount. The Black Duck Atlantic Coast Joint Venture Plan identifies the Narrow River estuary (which the plan refers to as "the Pettaquamscutt River") as the largest of 13 black duck focus areas in

Rhode Island. Annual midwinter black duck population trend surveys across Rhode Island have confirmed a steady, and marked, decline in numbers since the 1950's. Based on that trend information, black duck populations have declined by an estimated 83 percent in Rhode Island between 1950 and 1998 (USFWS 1998).

Other common salt marsh species found on the refuge include sharp-tailed sparrows and red-winged blackbirds. Snowy egrets are often found foraging in tidal channels and salt marsh pools. There is at least one osprey nest in the watershed and as many as three pairs forage there.

The uplands contain a diversity of nesting and migratory songbirds, including common yellowthroat, eastern pewee, gray catbird, common grackle, American redstart, blue-winged warbler, and white-eyed vireo.

Invertebrates, Reptiles, Amphibians, and Mammals

No surveys have been conducted for these species on refuge lands. The Narrow River Special Area Management Plan lists vertebrate species common to the Narrow River estuary.

Fish

Seventy-five species of fish have been documented to use the Narrow River at some point in their life history; 28 fish species and 5 shellfish species use the lower section of the river adjacent to the refuge (RI CRMC 1998). Appendix A identifies trust fish species using the watershed. The Narrow River provides the largest alewife run of any river in Rhode Island (RI CRMC 1998).

Cultural Resources

No archeological sites have been recorded on the refuge, but it is considered highly sensitive for both prehistoric and historic archeological resources.

Public Use

We have not monitored public use at Chafee Refuge; we estimate the number of visitors at 5,000 annually. Saltwater fishing was officially opened on the refuge, in accordance with State laws, through a Federal Register Notice in 1998 (50 CFR 32). The refuge has not been officially opened to any other public use. In general, monitoring and enforcement of public use policy is difficult because the entire refuge boundary has not been posted. Visitors and refuge staff alike are not always certain whether they are on refuge lands. Although Chafee Refuge has not been opened officially to any activity but fishing, the refuge still gets visitors. Known public use activities vary seasonally, but include wildlife-dependent activities such as birding, nature observation and photography, and recreational fishing.

There are only a few vantage points within Pettaquamscutt Cove, and the most accessible ones are on private land. Popular viewing spots are the Town of Narragansett nature trail at the south end of the Cove near South County Museum, the Middle Bridge pull-out, and the Sprague bridge on Route 1A where it crosses the neck of the Narrow River inlet. Two waterfowl hunting blinds adjacent to refuge lands in the cove may cause some activities incidental to hunting (e.g., retrieving birds) on refuge lands, but none have been documented.

Non-wildlife-dependent activities suspected of impacting the refuge include canoeing, kayaking, and using motor boats and jet skis. Motorized water craft operating in State waters within the cove likely contribute to shoreline erosion and disturb wildlife.

The refuge has no public use facilities. Incidental use occurs on several unimproved trails that access the shoreline. Several residents adjacent to Chafee Refuge have a legal easement to go across the refuge from their properties to the Narrow River. Ideally, refuge staff would like to consolidate these easements into a location that will reduce impact to sensitive areas along the shoreline.

The RI Department of Transportation is developing a South County Bike Path along 7.2 miles of the old Narragansett Pier Railroad, which crosses the refuge. The bike path will connect the towns of South Kingstown and Narragansett, and will be designed to accommodate cyclists, in-line skaters, walkers, joggers, and skateboarders. A swath up to 40 feet wide will be cleared for the 12-foot wide asphalt path. Its design is based on an expected peak of 400 users a day.

The Town of South Kingstown owns most of the old railroad right-of-way. The first segment connects Kingston train station to Peace Dale; the second segment connects Peace Dale to Wakefield; the third segment links Wakefield to Narragansett; and the fourth links Sprague Park to the Narragansett coast.

The proposed location of the third segment crosses approximately 600 feet of refuge land. Refuge staff and the RI DOT are now discussing design alternatives to minimize impacts to refuge lands. They have not yet reached a conclusion.

Chapter 4

Redstart
USFWS photo

Management Direction

- Refuge Complex Vision
- Refuge Complex Goals
- General Refuge Management

Refuge Complex Vision

We developed this vision statement to provide a guiding philosophy and sense of purpose for the five refuge CCPs. It qualitatively describes the desired future character of the Refuge Complex through 2015 and beyond. We wrote in the present tense to provide a more motivating, positive, and compelling statement of purpose. It has guided, and will continue to guide, program emphases and priorities for each refuge in Rhode Island.

"The Rhode Island National Wildlife Refuge Complex protects a unique collection of thriving coastal sandplain, coastal maritime, and beach strand communities, and represents some of the last undeveloped seacoast in southern New England. Leading the way in the protection and restoration of coastal wetlands, shrubland, and grassland habitats, the Refuge Complex contributes to the long-term conservation of migratory and resident native wildlife populations, and the recovery of endangered and threatened species. These refuges offer research opportunities and provide an outstanding showcase of habitat management for other landowners."

"The Refuge Complex is the premiere destination for visitors to coastal Rhode Island to engage in high quality, wildlife-dependent recreation. Hundreds of thousands of visitors are rewarded each year with inspiring vistas and exceptional opportunities to view wildlife in native habitats. Innovative environmental educational and interpretive programs motivate visitors to become better stewards of coastal resources."

"Through partnerships and extensive outreach efforts, Refuge Complex staff are committed to accomplishing refuge goals and significantly contributing to the Mission of the National Wildlife Refuge System. This commitment will strengthen with the future, revitalizing the southern New England ecosystem for generations to come."

Refuge Complex Goals

Our planning team developed the following goals for the Refuge Complex after reviewing applicable laws and policies, regional plans, the Refuge Complex vision statement, the purpose of each refuge, and public comments. All the goals fully comply with Service policy and national and regional mandates.

Our Refuge Complex goals are intentionally broad, descriptive statements of purpose. They highlight specific elements of our vision statement and provide the foundation for our management emphasis. We identified Goal 1 as the top priority for the Refuge Complex; Goals 2-5 are not presented in any particular order.

Each goal is further refined by a series of objective statements. Objectives are incremental steps to be taken toward achieving a goal and define the management emphasis in measurable terms, where possible. Some of our objectives relate directly to habitat management, while others strive to meet population targets tied to species' recovery plans, or state or regional species plans. The strategies for each objective are specific actions, tools, techniques, considerations, or a combination of these, which may be used to achieve the objective. Objectives will be used directly in respective step-down plans, while strategies may be revised or modified to achieve the desired outcome.

Together, the goals and objectives are unifying elements of successful refuge management. They identify and focus management priorities, provide a context for resolving issues, and offer a critical link between refuge purpose(s), and the National Wildlife Refuge System Mission.

Integral to all the objectives under Goal 1 and Goal 2 is development in 2003 of a habitat management plan (HMP) for the Refuge Complex. This will be the highest priority step-down plan to accomplish. We will write the plan using current resource information, but will update it based on new information, as needed. The purpose of the HMP will be to prevent the loss or degradation of habitat types, species assemblages, or natural processes significant to the Refuge Complex. It will identify habitat management actions that, to the extent practicable, restore and sustain viable populations of our focus species. The objectives and strategies identified below will all be incorporated into the HMP.

Once the HMP is developed, the Refuge Complex will develop a Species and Habitat Inventory and Monitoring Plan in 2004. Critical elements of the biological program to be inventoried or monitored will be identified, prioritized, and scheduled. This plan will also describe inventory and monitoring procedures, determine where data will be stored, and identify the interim and final reports to include. It will provide a critical connection between the HMP and credible, adaptive refuge management.

In addition, the Region is currently developing a strategic resources plan (SRP). This plan will establish Regional goals and objectives for species and habitats based on landscape-scale analyses. Each refuge staff will then determine their respective refuge's contribution to implementing these objectives. Once the SRP is completed, the objectives and strategies outlined below may be modified.

The following goals, objectives, and strategies provide management direction for the refuge over the next 15 years. Unless otherwise noted, all work will be accomplished by the Service, primarily by Refuge Complex staff.

Goal 1: Protect and enhance federal trust resources and other species and habitats of special concern.

Objective 1.1
Maintain high quality wintering and nesting habitat for American black duck and other native, migratory waterfowl on Chafee Refuge through management of public use and the control of invasive, non-native plant and animal species.

Background:
Chafee Refuge was established primarily to protect and enhance the populations of black ducks and other waterfowl. The 1986 North American Waterfowl Management Plan (NAWMP) identified the American black duck as a priority species of "immediate international concern." This plan considers the protection of essential migrating

and wintering habitat vitally important. The NAWMP's Atlantic Coast Joint Venture Plan identifies the Narrow River estuary, including Chafee Refuge, as the largest of 13 Black Duck Focus Areas in Rhode Island. Mid-winter waterfowl counts on the Narrow River, conducted annually by the State since the late 1950's, continue to document some of the highest concentrations of wintering black duck in Rhode Island. Bufflehead, hooded and common merganser, and canvasback mid-winter numbers are also high for the State.

Unfortunately, the waterfowl habitat is threatened by invasions of non-native plants and animals such as *Phragmites* and mute swan, poor water quality, and by increased recreational pressures. Invasive species are a threat because they displace native plants and animals, reduce natural diversity, and degrade habitat conditions for our focus species. Poor water quality, as evidenced by increased coliform bacteria and nitrogen levels, impacts food resources for waterfowl in the river. The increased recreational pressure may be directly impacting black duck and other native waterfowl, especially when it occurs during nesting and brooding seasons.

Treatments to control invasive species and improve water quality are expensive and labor intensive and will require extensive partnerships with adjacent landowners, State and Federal agencies, and the local governments. The 1998 Narrow River Special Area Management Plan (SAMP) identifies specific actions for addressing these issues through interagency cooperation (also refer to objectives 2.3 and 2.4). The Service will specifically work with RI DEM to develop recommendations to improve habitat quality for black duck and other native, wintering and nesting waterfowl.

Strategies:

■ By 2003, treat at least 5 acres per year of *Phragmites* or other invasive wetland plants on the refuge through mechanical, chemical, or biological treatments to improve habitat for black duck and other waterfowl (also see objective 2.3).

■ In 2003, work with RI DEM and respective towns to develop a Pettaquamscutt Cove (lower Narrow River) waterfowl management area plan. Evaluate and designate waterfowl resting areas, habitat restoration opportunities, and hunting opportunities. Establish management actions to attain zero productivity of mute swan.

Objective 1.2
Within two years of CCP completion, establish specific habitat management objectives for those birds considered by Partners In Flight (PIF) to be a high conservation priority in PIF Area 9, Southern New England, and for which the refuge could make an important contribution to their conservation.

Background:
PIF Bird Conservation Plans are written for physiographic provinces with an overall goal to ensure the long term maintenance of healthy populations of landbirds. These plans identify species and habitats most in need of conservation, describe desired habitat conditions for these species, develop biological objectives, and recommend conservation actions. Rhode Island Refuges lie within PIF Area 9.

Although the final PIF Area 9 plan is not yet available, this CCP incorporates habitat objectives for certain landbird species identified in the draft PIF plan (Oct 2000) which occur on the refuge (also see objective 1.3). Using information from the surveys identified below, and the completed PIF plan, we will be able to refine our refuge landbird management objectives in the near future.

Of particular note is the refuge staff's involvement in monitoring a piping plover (Federal-listed as threatened) nesting area on Town of Narragansett lands. The nesting area is located at the end of the Narragansett Town Beach, where a wide sandy area has formed at the mouth of the Narrow River. Piping plover have been documented nesting in this area since 1997. Also associated at this site are least tern (State-listed as threatened). Refuge staff monitor this site along with nine other piping plover nesting sites on RI's South Shore. For more information on Service involvement in the South Shore Piping Plover Program, refer to the Trustom Pond Refuge CCP (May 2002).

Strategies:

■ Each year, continue to cooperate with RI DEM, the Service's Ecological Services Program Office, and the Town of Narragansett in the monitoring of the Narrow River piping plover and least tern nest sites. Monitoring and management actions will meet or exceed the Service's 1994 Guidelines for Managing Recreational Activities in Piping Plover Breeding Habitat on the U.S. Atlantic Coast To Avoid take Under Section 9 of the Endangered Species Act (Appendix G in the 1996 Piping Plover Recovery Plan).

■ In 2003, utilize the PIF Area 9 Plan, and the regional strategic resources plan (in preparation), to identify and prioritize those landbirds of highest management concern on the refuge, and assess how current management practices are impacting them. Determine which of these landbirds should be a focus for future management on the refuge, and write landbird objectives for the HMP.

■ In conjunction with developing the HMP, update refuge cover type maps in a GIS database, adhering to National Vegetation Classification protocol.

■ Utilize the Shorebird Conservation Plan (once completed) to develop management and monitoring strategies for shorebirds based on any newly identified imperiled species (draft Shorebird Prioritization System 1999).

Objective 1.3
Protect and sustain marsh, wading and water bird breeding habitat on the refuge, especially maritime high salt marsh capable of supporting salt marsh sharp-tailed sparrow.

Background:
According to the PIF Area 9 Plan, maritime marsh is the habitat in most need of immediate conservation attention in this physiographic area, due to the large number of priority species and the tremendous pressure from human development along the coastline. Substantial threats also exist in the form of human disturbance, pollution,

increasing predator populations, and invasive, exotic species. Reducing these threats is the highest conservation concern to be addressed in the PIF plan. Active restoration of high salt marsh is also a priority.

No bird surveys have been conducted on the refuge. However, the 1998 Narrow River SAMP identifies the presence of breeding sharp-tailed sparrow, Virginia and clapper rail, and green heron in the area. Great blue, little blue, and black-crowned night heron, American bittern, great and snowy egret, and sora rail are all noted in the SAMP as present during migration or winter.

Strategies:

■ In 2003, begin to conduct salt-marsh sharp-tailed sparrow surveys in suitable habitat according to Regional protocol.

■ Use the North American Waterbird Conservation Plan (once completed) to identify management and monitoring strategies for species of conservation priority.

■ By 2005, initiate an inventory for all marsh and wading birds, according to Regional protocol, at all high probability sites. Determine seasonal occupancy and nesting status. If occupied habitat is located, develop a site plan.

Goal 2: Maintain and/or restore natural ecological communities to promote healthy, functioning ecosystems.

Objective 2.1
Within three years of CCP completion, design and implement a baseline inventory on refuge lands to determine the occurrence of species and habitats of management concern (Appendix A), and to serve as a basis for future management decisions.

Background:
To keep the HMP relevant, we will need to improve our general knowledge of important refuge resources, including their presence, distribution, and condition, to insure management actions are effective in sustaining biological integrity, diversity, and ecosystem health as required by Service policy (FWS Manual, Chapter 3, part 601).

As stated in the introduction for this chapter, a Species and Habitat Inventory and Monitoring Plan will be completed in 2004. The following strategies will be incorporated into this plan.

Strategies:

■ By 2004, develop a priority list of baseline biological inventory needs to better understand and document the biodiversity on the refuge, especially the presence and distribution of species and habitat types listed in Appendix A.

■ In 2004, begin inventories on the highest priority projects, incorporating the results into the CENSUS database, or other regional databases with GIS capabilities, to facilitate future analyses. Revise digital cover type maps as warranted.

Objective 2.2
Within 15 years of CCP completion, restore natural ecological conditions to the 74 acres of salt-marsh and other emergent wetlands on the refuge.

Background:
Wetlands are among the most productive ecosystems on earth, and salt marsh wetlands rank among the highest of wetlands, in terms of productivity. The tidal influence, including nutrient import, water abundance, and vegetative growth, all contribute to this productivity. Healthy wetlands function in ways that benefit the natural ecosystem and provide socio-economic values. Ecosystem values include the fact that certain fish, shellfish, birds, and mammals are wetland-dependent, spending their entire lives in these wetlands. Many waterfowl, wading birds, shorebirds, and other migratory birds utilize wetlands for feeding or resting, or to breed and raise their young. Wetlands are also essential habitats for many rare species of plants and animals. Wetlands function in ways that filter sediments and pollutants, produce oxygen, and support healthy microbiota for fish and wildlife. Socio-economic values include flood control, wave damage protection, hunting, trapping, fishing and shellfishing, aesthetics, education and research.

As noted in objective 1.3 above, maritime marsh is the habitat in most need of immediate conservation attention in this physiographic area due to the large number of priority species and the tremendous pressure from human development along the coastline. While we have identified restoration of only 74 acres on refuge lands, when coupled with the partnership effort described in objective 2.4, significant ecosystem and socio-economic benefits are expected.

Strategies:

■ By 2005, conduct inventory of wetland vegetation on the refuge according to Regional protocol. Develop digital map to serve as a baseline for future inventories and monitoring. Identify threats to refuge wetlands, including pollution sources, invasive plants, impediments to natural hydrology, and impacts from recreational activities.

■ By 2006, work with partners to identify, prioritize, and begin to implement wetlands restoration project on the refuge.

Objective 2.3
Within three years of CCP completion, treat at least 5 acres/year dominated by invasive, non-native plants to (1) enhance native habitat, (2) eliminate new invasions, and (3) control the spread of established plants.

Background:
Issue 5 in Chapter 1 describes the implications of invasive plants on the refuges. These plants are a threat because they displace native plant and animal species, degrade wetlands and other natural communities, and reduce natural diversity and wildlife habitat values. They outcompete native species and can readily dominate a site. Early detection and consistent efforts at eradication are critical to maintain control over affected areas, or to prevent new invasions.

Strategies:

- By 2004, identify and map current distribution of non-native, invasive plant species on the refuge.

- By 2005, prioritize treatment sites to prevent new invasions or eradicate recently established plants. Also of high priority are threatened, endangered, or rare plant sites or "pristine rare and exemplary vegetative communities" (March 1999 Invasive Plant Control Initiative, Strategic Plan for the Connecticut River Watershed/Long Island Sound).

- By 2005, establish a program to treat at least 5 acres/year of invasive, non-native species on the refuge, using chemical, mechanical, prescribed fire and biological treatments as necessary. Strategies will be adapted based on monitoring and new information. A maintenance worker will be hired to administer treatments; the position will be shared among the five Rhode Island refuges.

Objective 2.4
Work in partnership to promote stewardship of the Lower Narrow River Watershed, including Pettaquamscutt Cove, and improve water quality, anadromous fish habitat, and other wetlands values by identifying and reducing pollution sources.

Background:
The Narrow River, including Pettaquamscutt Cove, is an incredibly important natural resource benefitting both wildlife and people in the South County area. At least 75 species of fish are supported by the area at some point during their life history. The Narrow River provides the largest alewife run of any Rhode Island river (RI CRMC 1998). Other resource and socio-economic values attributed to wetlands are described in objective 2. 2. Unfortunately, water quality in the Narrow River continues to fall below state standards with development and recreational pressures remaining high.

Because areas below mean high water are the jurisdiction of the State, the Service has only an indirect influence on the water and tidal shoreline. It is primarily the Coastal Zone Management Council (CRMC) that has regulatory authority. Through development of SAMPs, the CRMC coordinates with other inland regulatory authorities to take a comprehensive approach to management of the watershed. In their 1998 Narrow River SAMP, the CRMC recommended an interagency working group of non-profit, State, Federal, and municipal representatives. This group would formulate a comprehensive plan for the watershed based on existing scientific data. The plan would describe best management practices to address storm drain outfalls, identify habitat restoration possibilities, identify important fish habitats, and recommend actions to curtail bacteria and nitrogen sources not addressed by existing regulations. Along with other actions noted below, the Service will become an active participant in this working group.

Strategies:

- In 2003, work with RI DEM, RI CRMC, and the Towns of Narragansett and South Kingstown to create a "no wake" zone in Pettaquamscutt Cove and the lower Narrow River to reduce erosion and destruction of salt marshes on the refuge.

■ By 2005, work toward watershed-based solutions to the water quality problems impacting the Narrow River. We will become actively involved in an interagency working group, as recommended in RI CRMC's 1998 Narrow River SAMP. This interagency working group will be organized to develop a comprehensive plan for the Narrow River watershed and to set research and management priorities.

■ Also by 2005, refuge staff will become involved in the South County Watershed Partnership to promote protection and stewardship of watersheds influencing the refuges.

■ By 2006, identify watershed restoration projects for refuge lands; also described in objective 2.2 and 2.3.

Objective 2.5
Within 15 years of CCP implementation, eliminate mute swan productivity on the refuge, and significantly reduce the presence of adults year-round.

Background:
Non-native, invasive mute swan on the refuge adversely effect water quality on coastal ponds. Mute swan also impact our ability to maintain native species biodiversity, as they aggressively drive native waterfowl and shorebirds away from nesting sites and compete with them for food resources.

Strategies:

■ In 2002, we will begin to implement the Service's policy (Memo FWS/MBMO/98-00043; based on Flyway Council recommendations) to significantly reduce or eliminate mute swans on the refuge. Strategies will be adapted as needed to pursue zero productivity. Each year, addling eggs will continue. Adult populations will be controlled using lethal and non-lethal techniques, particularly when habitat degradation is a concern, or if native species are displaced.

Objective 2.6
Within two years of CCP completion, develop a deer management plan for the Refuge Complex to address overabundant deer populations and evaluate recreational hunting opportunities.

Background:
Overabundant deer numbers are a concern on the refuge when they degrade habitat through excessive browsing or threaten human health and safety through increased vehicle collisions and incidences of Lyme disease. Since deer are highly mobile, it is difficult to effectively control a population unless they are managed throughout most or all of their range. The refuge has not closely monitored deer activities, including their impacts to refuge habitats. However, RI DEM has reported that complaints from citizens have increased in recent years about private property damage, worries of Lyme disease, and vehicle collisions. RI DEM recommends deer hunting as the most effective tool to manage deer populations on the refuge.

Strategies:

■ In 2002, cooperate with RI DEM to develop a deer management plan and environmental assessment for the Refuge Complex. The plan will evaluate hunting to help manage deer numbers and provide a priority public use opportunity. A separate public involvement process will be initiated.

Map 4-1

John H. Chafee at Pettaquamscutt Cove National Wildlife Refuge

Public Use/Habitat Improvements

Comprehensive Conservation Plan

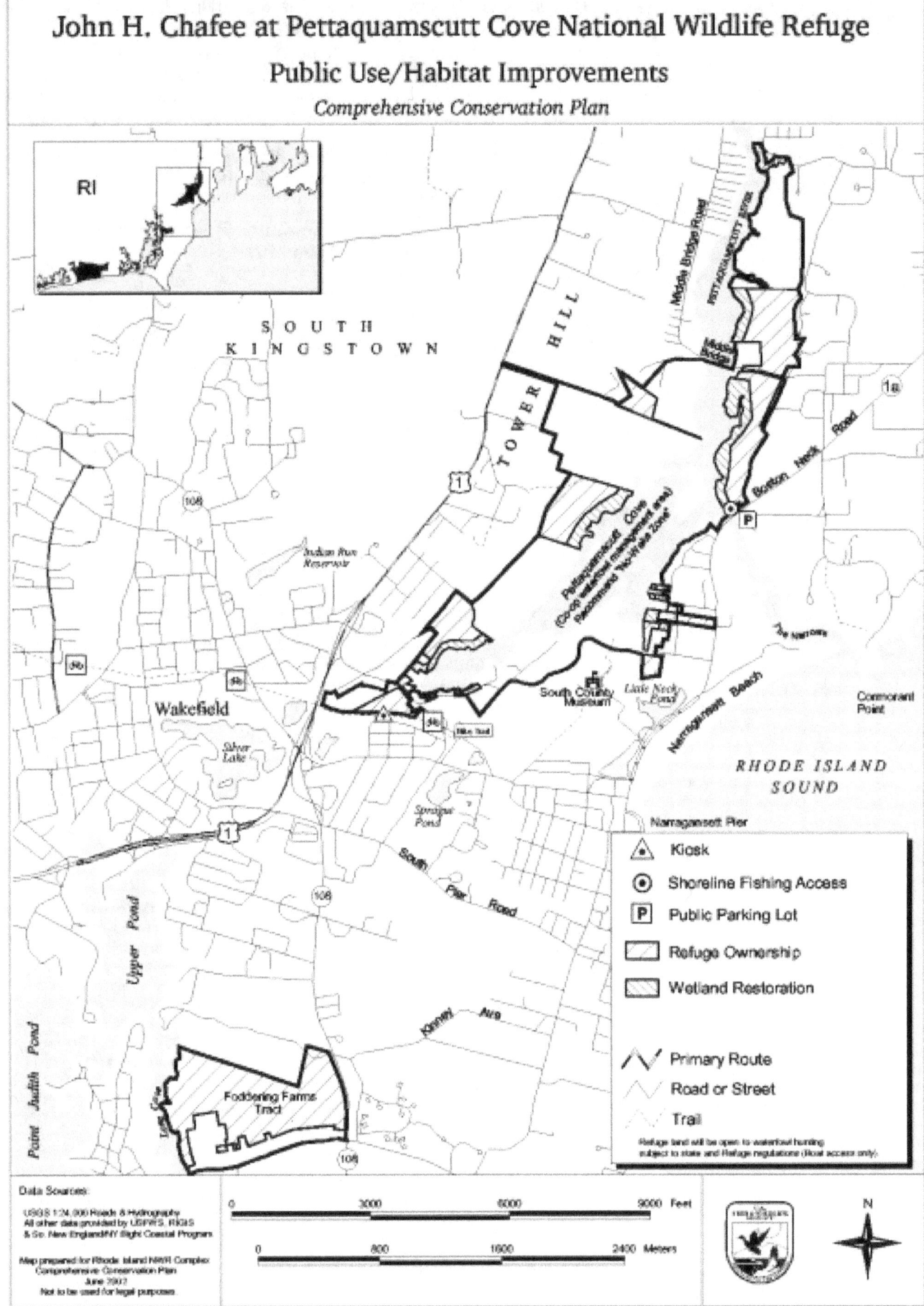

⚠	Kiosk
◉	Shoreline Fishing Access
P	Public Parking Lot
▨	Refuge Ownership
▨	Wetland Restoration
∿	Primary Route
∿	Road or Street
∿	Trail

Refuge land will be open to waterfowl hunting
subject to state and Refuge regulations (Boat access only).

Data Sources:

USGS 1:24,000 Roads & Hydrography
All other data provided by USFWS, RIGIS
& So. New England/NY Bight Coastal Program.

Map prepared for Rhode Island NWR Complex
Comprehensive Conservation Plan
June 2002
Not to be used for legal purposes.

0   3000   6000   9000 Feet

0   800   1600   2400 Meters

N

Goal 3: Establish a land protection program that fully supports accomplishment of species, habitat, and ecosystem goals.

Objective 3.1
Actively strive towards permanent protection of all trust resources at risk throughout southern Rhode Island.

Background:
Consistently mentioned in the PIF Area 9 Plan, the NAWMP, joint venture plans, relevant species recovery plans, and ecosystem plans is the need to protect, restore, and enhance additional high quality coastal habitats to contribute to the conservation of federal trust species. While land acquisition by the Service and other State, Federal, and local partners is a primary strategy for species conservation, each of these plans also recognizes the need to work in cooperation with private landowners to achieve conservation objectives. Technical and resource support, outreach, and education will all compliment land acquisition efforts.

The Draft CCP/EA (Chapter 3: Developing Land Protection Strategies) described our method of identifying acquisition lands of high conservation priority on Rhode Island's South Shore. During the planning process we determined that the Service is the logical leader in coastal land and water quality protection along the South Shore and on Block Island, with the existing refuges serving as anchors. Refuge expansions will significantly increase protection of the ecological values on current refuge lands, while also expanding protection and restoration of significant coastal habitats. We completed a Land Protection Plan for the Refuge Complex which identifies specific tracts for Service acquisition. The LPP incorporates the following acquisition priorities:

- Has documented occurrences of federally listed endangered or threatened species, or other priority federal trust resources;

- Lies contiguous to existing refuge land, which could further enhance or protect the integrity of refuges by assembling the land base necessary to accomplish refuge goals;

- Connects refuge land with other protected lands withing the South Shore and Block Island to help restore and promote the ecological integrity of the coastal wetland and beach strand complexes; and

- Protects and sustains important natural communities that can be managed in cooperation with other conservation partners in a manner that will contribute toward refuge goals and the conservation of federal trust resources.

Strategies:

- Continue to assist conservation partners in identifying land protection needs, opportunities, and priorities in southern Rhode Island.

- Continue to help partners seek funding sources for their land protection programs.

- Beginning in 2002, expand the refuge acquisition boundary for Chafee Refuge according to the Land Protection Plan (Appendix E). Initiate acquisition from willing sellers, in either fee purchase or conservation easement, of 1,013 acres of high quality habitat.

Goal 4: Provide opportunities for high quality, compatible, wildlife-dependent public use with particular emphasis on environmental education and interpretation.

Integral to all of our public use objectives is development of a Visitor Services Plan in 2004 for the Refuge Complex. This plan will provide a coordinated strategy for implementing quality visitor services programs. We will emphasize the following six priority, wildlife-dependent uses identified in the 1997 Refuge Improvement Act where they are compatible with protecting wildlife resources: hunting, fishing, wildlife observation and photography, environmental education and interpretation. The visitor services plan will also accomplish the following:

- Establish strategic goals and priorities for visitor services across the Refuge Complex;

- Identify target audiences and partnership opportunities for each refuge;

- Establish a methodology for determining visitor numbers, capacity limits, limits on visitor impacts to wildlife and habitats, and a means for assessing quality of visitor experiences;

- Evaluate recreational fee opportunities; and

- Establish an implementation schedule for priority visitor services projects.

We will hire four outdoor recreation planners to implement the visitor services plan and staff the planned Refuge Complex Visitor Center (see Chapter 5- Staffing). As new lands are acquired, opportunities to provide compatible, priority public uses will be pursued according to the Pre-Acquisition Compatibility Determination (Appendix D).

The objectives below are designed to enhance opportunities for compatible, wildlife-dependent refuge activities.

Objective 4.1
Within two years of CCP completion, provide high quality waterfowl hunting opportunities in the Pettaquamscutt Cove area of the refuge, and evaluate opportunities for deer hunting across the refuge.

Strategies:

- In 2002, complete a deer management plan and environmental assessment evaluating opportunities for deer hunting. A separate public involvement process will be initiated. (Also refer to objective 2.6)

- By 2003, develop hunt plan and fulfill other Service requirements to open Chafee Refuge to waterfowl hunting, including associated dog retrieval, for the fall 2003 season. Hunting will be administered according to state and local regulations, and will be by boat access only. Additional refuge regulations may be determined necessary during development of the hunt plan. The hunt program will be administered in cooperation with RI DEM.

Objective 4.2
Provide high quality fishing opportunities along the refuge shoreline, while minimizing impacts to natural resources.

Strategies:

■ Continue to allow fishing from boats and the shoreline, but by 2005, designate a trail to provide overland access to shoreline fishing areas; minimize further bank erosion and trampling of marsh habitat and other sensitive areas; and avoid trespassing on private lands.

■ By 2007, construct at least one barrier-free fishing platform on refuge lands, if technically feasible. Otherwise, consider cooperative project with RI DEM or adjacent landowners on private or state lands near the refuge.

Objective 4.3
Increase opportunities for high quality interpretive experiences on the refuge, which raise visitor awareness of the Refuge System and Chafee Refuge's particular contribution to protecting trust resources and significant habitats.

Strategies:

■ Continue to respond to requests for interpretive programs using refuge staff and volunteers.

■ By 2003, ensure that RI DOT constructs interpretive kiosk on refuge along South County Bike Trail according to refuge stipulations.

■ By 2005, develop an interpretive program for the refuge tiered to the visitor services plan. Evaluate the opportunities to cooperate on an interpretive exhibit at South County Museum and construct an interpretive kiosk, pullout and accessible overlook at Middle Bridge.

■ By 2006, evaluate opportunities for constructing an interpretive kiosk and accessible trail and overlook at Bridgeport Commons.

■ By 2006, designate an interpretive canoe and kayak trail along the refuge shoreline.

Objective 4.4
Improve opportunities for compatible, high quality wildlife observation and photography on the refuge, while minimizing impacts to natural resources.

Strategies:

■ By 2005, cooperate with the Town of Narragansett, adjacent landowners, and RI DOT to evaluate opportunities to construct an accessible pullout and overlook at Middle Bridge.

■ By 2006, develop literature on seasonal wildlife observation and photography opportunities in the lower Narrow River.

■ Also by 2006, evaluate opportunities for constructing an accessible observation overlook and trail at Bridgeport Commons. The final trail would be located to avoid sensitive areas, minimize erosion and avoid trespassing on private lands.

■ Foot travel, snowshoeing, cross-country skiing, canoes and kayaks are approved means of access to engage in priority public use activities.

Objective 4.5
Create new opportunities for compatible, high quality environmental educational experiences on the refuge, while minimizing impacts to natural resources.

Strategies:

- By 2004, sponsor at least one "Teach the Teacher" workshop, and continue as an annual program.

- By 2005, with partners, develop an environmental education program tiered to the visitors services plan. Work with local schools to develop an outdoor-based curriculum featuring the Narrow River estuary and Pettaquamscutt Cove.

- Also by 2005, develop a formal partnership with South County Museum to conduct curriculum based environmental education programs.

Objective 4.6
Within three years of CCP completion, eliminate incompatible, non-wildlife dependent public uses on the refuge.

Background:
Incompatible, non-wildlife dependent activities detract from our ability to fulfill refuge purposes and often conflict with priority public uses. None of these uses are necessary for the safe, practical, or effective conduct of a priority public use, and in fact, are often disruptive to priority public uses. Limited refuge resources should not be expended to manage activities that do not contribute to the public's understanding and appreciation of the refuge's wildlife or cultural resources, or to activities that do not directly benefit these resources.

Strategies:

- By 2004, increase resource protection and management of public use by utilizing law enforcement personnel to provide more consistent and thorough outreach and enforcement of refuge regulations.

- By 2004, hire at least one additional law enforcement officer for the Refuge Complex.

Goal 5: Provide refuge staffing, operations, and maintenance support to effectively accomplish refuge goals and objectives.

Staffing, operations, and maintenance needs are addressed in Chapter 5.

General Refuge Management Direction

The following management direction applies to all of the refuge goals and across all program areas. Some of this direction is required by Service policy or legal mandates.

Maintaining Biological Integrity, Diversity, and Environmental Health

The Service finalized its policy on Maintaining the Biological Integrity, Diversity, and Environmental Health of the National Wildlife Refuge System in January 2001 (FWS manual, Part 601, Chapter 3). This policy directs us, first and foremost, to maintain existing levels of biological integrity, diversity, and environmental health on refuges. Secondarily, we will restore lost or severely degraded elements of integrity, diversity, and environmental health on refuges where it is feasible and supports refuge purpose(s). To implement the policy on refuges, refuge managers are directed to determine: each refuge's relationship between refuge purpose(s) and biological integrity, diversity, and environmental health; what conditions constitute biological integrity, diversity, and environmental health; how to maintain existing levels of all three; and how, and when to appropriately restore lost elements of all three (Chapter 3, section 3.9)

The objectives and strategies laid out in this CCP generally improve the biological integrity, diversity, and environmental health of the refuge. Management actions emphasize maintaining current species and habitat diversity, recovering endangered and threatened species, and restoring natural ecosystem processes and functions. Implementation of the CCP will increase our understanding of the refuge's current resources, sustainable natural conditions, and the effects of our management actions. In addition, our strategy of adaptive management will provide continuous improvement toward meeting this policy's intent.

Protecting and Managing Cultural Resources

By law, we must consider the effects of our actions on archeological and historic resources. We will comply with Section 106 of the National Historic Preservation Act before disturbing any ground. Compliance may require any or all of the following: a State historic preservation records survey, literature survey, or field survey.

In addition to basic compliance requirements, we will undertake the following projects to better protect and interpret cultural resources on the refuge:

- By 2005, initiate a cultural resources overview of the Refuge Complex to increase the available data on cultural resources.

- Also by 2005, develop a Memorandum of Understanding (MOU) with the Narragansett Indian Tribal Council to facilitate cooperation on environmental education and interpretation, to improve our understanding of the context of natural resources, and to increase site identification and protection.

■ By 2006, train at least one law enforcement officer on the refuge in regulations associated with the Archeological Resources Protection Act (ARPA).

Tribal Coordination

Increasing communication with the Narragansett Indian Tribal Council is very important for the Refuge Complex. As noted above, we plan to develop an MOU by 2005 to establish a mutually beneficial working relationship that includes cooperating in environmental education and interpretation and protecting cultural resources.

Coastal Resources Management Council Coordination

The federal Coastal Zone Management Act (16 U.S.C. §1451, as amended) requires the Service to work with the State Coastal Resources Management Council (CRMC) to insure refuge programs and activities are consistent to the maximum extent practicable with the enforceable policies adopted by the state. The CRMC's concurrence with the Service's Federal Consistency Determination on the CCP was predicated on meeting the following management direction:

1) **Provide separate consistency determinations for major construction projects**. Major construction projects such as buildings, parking lots, roads, and boardwalks, which the Service determines may effect coastal resources, will require separate federal consistency determinations for each project.

2) **Annual coordination meetings**. Refuge Complex and CRMC staff will meet at least once annually to review general plans and projects which the Service has determined may effect coastal resources. These meetings will cover proposals for the forthcoming calendar year. The objective of these meetings will be to provide CRMC staff with available details on what is being proposed and to address their concerns. It is mutually understood that some projects may not be fully developed at the time of meeting.

Refuge Revenue Sharing Payments

Annual refuge revenue sharing payments to the Towns of South Kingstown and Narragansett will continue. Future increases in payments will be commensurate with increases in the appraised fair market values of refuge lands, new acquisitions of land, and new Congressional appropriations.

Controlling Mosquitos

Within the past few years, incidences of mosquito-borne Eastern Equine Encephalitis and West Nile virus have elevated public health concerns about mosquito control in the Middle Atlantic States. Mosquito control has been very limited on the Refuge Complex, and has occurred only at the direct request of the State's Mosquito Abatement Office. During the last 5 years, we used two very localized applications of the larvicide Bti on two problem breeding sites. Our regional contaminants specialist pre-approved those applications.

In general, we will not use larvicides on the Refuge Complex to control mosquitos. However, in cooperation with neighboring towns and the Mosquito Abatement Office, we will consider applying larvicides on a case-by-case basis, particularly when there is an elevated public health risk. The Service is now evaluating this issue on a regional basis, and has begun preparation for an environmental impact statement. This may result in Service policy or Regional guidelines being developed and incorporated into this CCP in the future.

Permitting Special Use (including Research)

Requests for special use permits will be evaluated by the refuge manager on a case-by-case. All permitted activities must be determined appropriate and compatible through a compatibility determination. At a minimum, all commercial activities and all research projects require a special use permit. Research projects that will improve and strengthen natural resource management decisions on the Refuge Complex will generally be approved. The refuge manager will encourage partnerships with local universities and colleges to facilitate research that will help evaluate CCP objectives and strategies, or the assumptions on which they are based.

The refuge manager may also consider research not directly related to refuge objectives, but which contributes to the broader enhancement, protection, or management of native species and biological diversity within the region.

Each refuge will maintain a list of research needs to provide prospective researchers or organizations upon request. The refuge manager will determine on a case-by-case basis whether they can directly support a project through funding, in-kind services (e.g. housing or use of other facilities), field assistance, or through sharing data and records. Research results will be shared within the Service, and with RI DEM.

All researchers on refuges, current and future, are required to submit a detailed research proposal following Service policy in the FWS Refuge Manual, Chapter 4 Section 6. Special use permits must also identify a schedule for progress reports (at least annual), criteria for determining when a project should cease, and publication or other final reporting requirements. The regional refuge biologists, other Service divisions, and state agencies will be asked to review and comment on research proposals.

Some projects, such as depredation and banding studies, require additional Service permits. These projects will not be approved until all Service permits and Endangered Species Act consultation requirements are met. Also, to maintain the natural landscape of the refuge, projects which require permanent or semi-permanent structures will not be allowed, except for extenuating circumstances unforseen at this time.

Chapter 5

Freshwater wetland
USFWS photo

Implementation and Monitoring

- Refuge Complex Staffing
- Refuge Complex Funding
- Step-down Management Plans
- Partnerships
- Volunteer Program
- Monitoring and Evaluation
- Adaptive Management
- Compatibility Determinations
- Additional NEPA Analysis
- Plan Amendment and Revision

Refuge Complex Staffing

The five Rhode Island Refuges are managed as a Refuge Complex, with centrally stationed staff taking on duties at multiple refuges. A total of 26 full time personnel, one Student-to-Career Experience Program (SCEP) trainee, and 17 seasonal personnel, are needed to fully implement all five Refuge CCPs. Permanent staff serving all five refuges may be stationed at the Refuge Headquarters in Charlestown, RI, or at Sachuest Point Refuge in Middletown, RI. Some permanent and temporary staff may be stationed seasonally on Block Island Refuge. Appendix G identifies currently filled positions, recommended new positions, and the overall supervisory structure. The new positions identified will increase visitor services, biological expertise, and visibility of the Service on refuge lands.

Refuge Complex Funding

Successful implementation of the CCPs for each refuge relies on our ability to secure funding, personnel, infrastructure, and other resources to accomplish the actions identified. Full implementation of the actions and strategies in all five Refuge Complex CCPs would incur one-time costs of $8.9 million. This includes staffing, major construction projects, and individual resource program expansions. Most of these projects have been identified as Tier 1 or Tier 2 Projects in the National Wildlife Refuge System's Refuge Operations Needs System database (RONS). Appendix F lists RONS projects and their recurring costs, such as salaries, following the first year. Also presented in Appendix F is a list of projects in the Service's current Maintenance Management System (MMS) database for the Refuge Complex. Currently, the MMS database lists $3.85 million in maintenance needs for the Refuge Complex.

Land acquisition costs are identified separately. The Land Protection Plan (LPP, Appendix E) expanded the Refuge Complex acquisition boundary by 2,681, increasing the total unacquired acreage to 3,130. We estimate the value of these lands to be $83 million at current, fair-market prices. In all probability, the Refuge Complex will protect these lands at a lower cost, as some parcels may be protected through conservation easements or acquired through donation or land exchange.

Step-Down Management Plans

The Refuge System Manual (Part 4 Chapter 3) lists more than 25 Step-Down Management Plans generally required on most refuges. Step-down plans describe specific management actions a refuge will follow to achieve objectives or implement management strategies. Some require annual revision, others are revised on a 5- to 10-year schedule. Some require additional NEPA analysis, public involvement, and compatibility determinations before they can be implemented. A status list of Rhode Island Refuge Complex step-down plans follows.

These plans are current :

■ Fire Management Plan, 1995 (Refuge Complex); updated with annual burn plans

■ Grasslands Management Plan, 1994 (Trustom Pond Refuge); will be incorporated into the Habitat Management Plan for the Refuge Complex in 2003

■ Continuity of Operations Plan, 1998 (Refuge Complex)

■ Animal Control Plan, 1995 (Refuge Complex); will be updated with Integrated Predator Management and Trapping Plans for the Refuge Complex

These plans are now in draft form or being prepared:

■ Safety Program and Operations Plan (Refuge Complex)

■ Law Enforcement Plan (Refuge Complex)

These plans exist, but we consider them out-of-date and needing revisions as indicated:

■ Water Management Plan (Trustom Pond Refuge); incorporate into Habitat Management Plan by 2003

■ Hunting Plan (Trustom Pond Refuge); incorporate into Hunt Plan for the Refuge Complex in 2003

■ Sign Plan (Refuge Complex); expand to Facilities and Sign Plan by 2005

■ Croplands Management Plan (Trustom Pond Refuge); incorporate into Habitat Management Plan for Refuge Complex in 2003

These step-down plans need to be initiated and will be completed by the indicated dates:

■ Refuge Complex Habitat Management Plan (highest priority step down plan) in 2003

■ Refuge Complex Hunt Plan in 2003

■ Refuge Complex Species and Habitat Inventory and Monitoring Plan in 2004

■ Integrated Predator Management Plan in 2004

■ Refuge Complex Visitor Services Plan in 2004

■ Fishing Plan by 2005

■ Trapping Plan by 2004

Partnerships

The Refuge Complex staff is proud of its long history of partnerships. More than 45 partnerships have supported the refuges, including four universities and colleges, numerous departments within Rhode Island State government, town administrations, conservation commissions, school districts, conservation groups and land trusts, environmental education centers, historic preservation groups, adjacent landowners, and other federal agencies. These partnerships have resulted in biological research, cooperative management of threatened and endangered species and declining habitats, protection of open space, and environmental education programs.

Refuge staff were particularly delighted by the establishment in 1998 of a "Friends of the National Wildlife Refuges of Rhode Island" group. The Friends are a non-profit advocacy group dedicated to supporting Refuge Complex goals within the community through public education and interpretation, project funding, and volunteer coordination. Their mission is "...[to be] devoted to the conservation and development of needed healthy habitat for flora and fauna at the National Wildlife Refuges of Rhode Island and to the provision of a safe, accessible ecological experience for our visitors...."

We will strengthen and formalize refuge partnerships to promote coordinated management and facilitate sharing of resources. Our partnership with the Friends Group is vitally important to us for community relations and for support in implementing our resource programs. Partnerships help us build support for the refuge, facilitate the sharing of information, and supplement the efforts of refuge staff.

Strategies:
■ By 2003, we will conduct at least semi-annual meetings with the Friends Group to promote communication and evaluate implementation of the MOU. We will continue to actively support and promote the Friends Group's vital efforts in funding and implementing outreach and environmental education programs, which enhance our ability to meet refuge goals.

■ By 2005, develop formal agreements with current partners, such as the South County Tourism Council, local land trusts, and conservation organizations, to identify mutual goals, and opportunities for cost sharing, technical exchange and environmental education and interpretation.

Volunteer Program

Volunteers are vital to accomplishing all Refuge Complex goals. For example, in fiscal years 2000 and 2001, volunteers donated 9,332 and 10,000 hours respectively, assisting in environmental education programs, monitoring public use, maintaining facilities, and managing habitats. This translates to more than $110,000 worth of services contributed to the refuges in 2000 and $117,900 in 2001. Volunteers are also largely responsible for staffing the visitor contact station at Trustom Pond Refuge.

In 1999 we hired a permanent staff Volunteer Coordinator to improve the quality of the program through better coordination, supervision and training of volunteers, and to better integrate volunteers into all refuge programs. The coordinator compiles and distributes a quarterly newsletter to volunteers, refuge partners, and interest groups, keeping them informed about management activities and upcoming interpretive programs on the Refuge Complex.

Maintaining Existing Facilities

Periodic maintenance of existing facilities is critical to ensure safety and accessibility for Refuge Complex staff and visitors. Existing facilities include the Trustom Pond Refuge visitor contact station, Refuge Complex maintenance compound, and numerous parking areas, observation platforms, and trails. Many of these facilities are not currently Americans With Disabilities Act (ADA) compliant; upgrading is needed. Appendix F displays the fiscal year (FY) 2000 Maintenance Management System (MMS) database list of backlogged maintenance entries for the Refuge Complex.

We will also undertake the following strategies to improve the visibility of the Service:

■ By 2003, meet with RI DOT to modify existing U.S. Route 1 directional signs. At a minimum, propose changes to the existing sign directing visitors "To Moonstone Beach".

■ By 2005, complete construction of the Visitor Center/Headquarters for the Refuge Complex, implementing recommendations for interior facility design from the August 1999 Project Identification Document. At least one Visitor Services Specialist will be hired to administer the new facility.

■ By 2005, complete a Refuge Complex Facilities and Sign Plan.

Monitoring and Evaluation

Monitoring and Evaluation for this CCP will occur at two levels. The first level, which we refer to as implementation monitoring, responds to the question, "Did we do what we said we would do, when we said we would do it?" Annual implementation monitoring will be achieved by using the checklist in Appendix H for the Refuge Complex.

The second level of monitoring, which we refer to as effectiveness monitoring, responds to the question, "Are the actions we proposed effective in achieving the results we had hoped for?" Or, in other words, "Are the actions leading us toward our vision, goals, and objectives?" Effectiveness monitoring evaluates an individual action, a suite of actions, or an entire resource program. This approach is more analytical in evaluating management effects on species, populations, habitats, refuge visitors, ecosystem integrity, or the socio-economic environment. More often, the criteria to monitor and evaluate these management effects will be established in step-down, individual project, or cooperator plans, or through the research program. The Species and Habitat Inventory and Monitoring Plan, to be completed in 2004, will be based on the needs and priorities identified in the Habitat Management Plan.

Adaptive Management

This CCP is a dynamic document. A strategy of adaptive management will keep it relevant and current. Through scientific research, inventories and monitoring, and our management experiences, we will gain new information which may alter our course of action. We acknowledge that our information on species, habitats, and ecosystems is incomplete, provisional, and subject to change as our knowledge base improves.

Objectives and strategies must be adaptable in responding to new information and spatial and temporal changes. We will continually evaluate management actions, through monitoring or research, to reconsider whether their original assumptions and predictions are still valid. In this way, management becomes an active process of learning "what really works". It is important that the public understand and appreciate the adaptive nature of natural resource management.

The Refuge Manager is responsible for changing management actions or objectives if they do not produce the desired conditions. Significant changes may warrant additional NEPA analysis; minor changes will not, but will be documented in annual monitoring, project evaluation reports, or the annual refuge narratives.

Compatibility Determinations

Federal law and policy provide the direction and planning framework to protect the Refuge System from incompatible or harmful human activities and to insure that Americans can enjoy Refuge System lands and waters. The National Wildlife Refuge System Administration Act of 1966, as amended by the National Wildlife Refuge System Improvement Act of 1997, is the key legislation on managing public uses and compatibility.

Before activities or uses are allowed on a National Wildlife Refuge, we must determine that each is a "compatible use." A compatible use is a use that, based on the sound professional judgement of the Refuge Manager, " ...will not materially interfere with or detract from the fulfillment of the mission of the Refuge System or the purposes of the refuge." "Wildlife-dependent recreational uses may be authorized on a refuge when they are compatible and not inconsistent with public safety. Except for consideration of consistency with State laws and regulations as provided for in section (m), no other determinations or findings are required to be made by the refuge official under this Act or the Refuge Recreation Act for wildlife-dependent recreation to occur." (Refuge Improvement Act)

Compatibility determinations were distributed (in the draft CCP/EA) for a 51 day public review in early 2001. These determinations have since been approved, and will allow the continuation of the following public use programs: wildlife observation and photography, environmental education and interpretation, fishing, and hunting. A pre-acquisition compatibility determination was also reviewed and completed, and identifies which existing public uses would be allowed to continue on new properties acquired by the Refuge complex. Since releasing the draft CCP/EA, we have also distributed compatibility determinations for trapping and waterfowl hunting for a public review period. All comments were considered and utilized in the revision. These new compatibility determinations are now final and included in Appendix D.

Additional compatibility determinations will be developed when appropriate new uses are proposed. Compatibility determinations will be re-evaluated by the Refuge Manager when conditions under which the use is permitted change significantly; when there is significant new information on effects of the use; or at least every 10 years for non-priority public uses. Priority public use compatibility determinations will be re-evaluated under the conditions noted above, or at least every 15 years with revision of the CCP. Additional detail on the compatibility determination process is in Parts 25, 26, and 29 of Title 50 of the Code of Federal Regulations, effective November 17, 2000.

Additional NEPA Analysis

The National Environmental Policy Act (NEPA) requires a site-specific analysis of impacts for all federal actions. These impacts are to be disclosed in either an EA or Environmental Impact Statement (EIS).

Most of the actions and associated impacts in this plan were described in enough detail in the draft CCP/EA to comply with NEPA, and will not require additional environmental analysis. Although this is not an all-inclusive list, the following programs are examples that fall into this category: protecting piping plover, restoring area-defined grasslands and wetlands, implementing priority wildlife-dependent public use programs (except deer hunting), acquiring land, and controlling invasive plants.

Other actions are not described in enough detail to comply with the site-specific analysis requirements of NEPA. Examples of actions that will require a separate EA include: construction of a new visitor center and headquarters, new deer hunting opportunities, and future wetlands restoration projects not fully developed or delineated in this document. Monitoring, evaluation, and research can generally be increased without additional NEPA analysis.

Plan Amendment and Revision

Periodic review of the CCP will be required to ensure that objectives are being met and management actions are being implemented. Ongoing monitoring and evaluation will be an important part of this process. Monitoring results or new information may indicate the need to change our strategies.

The Service's planning policy (FWS Manual, Part 602, Chapters 1, 3, and 4) states that CCPs should be reviewed at least annually to decide if they require any revisions (Chapter 3, part 3.4 (8)). Revisions will be necessary if significant new information becomes available, ecological conditions change, major refuge expansions occur, or when we identify the need to do so during a program review. At a minimum, CCPs will be fully revised every 15 years. We will modify the CCP documents and associated management activities as needed, following the procedures outlined in Service policy and NEPA requirements. Minor revisions that meet the criteria for categorical exclusions (550 FW 3.3C) will only require an Environmental Action Statement.